TREASURE PALACES

TREASURE PALACES

GREAT WRITERS VISIT GREAT MUSEUMS

FOREWORD BY NICHOLAS SEROTA

EDITED BY MAGGIE FERGUSSON

Published under exclusive licence from The Economist by Profile Books Ltd
3 Holford Yard
Bevin Way
London WC1X 9HD
www.profilebooks.com

Illustrations by Steve Panton

Text design by *amanda.brookes@brookesforty.com*
Typeset in Albertina by MacGuru Ltd

Printed and bound in Great Britain by Clays, St Ives plc

A CIP catalogue record for this book is available from the British Library

ISBN 978 1 78125 690 9
eISBN 978 1 78283 278 2

Contents

Foreword

Museums are the places in which we can discover the past, reflect on our understanding of the world and gain insights that will guide us into the future. It was T. S. Eliot who reminded us that

> Time present and time past
> Are both perhaps present in time future

and that our understanding of "the past should be altered by the present, as much as the present is directed by the past".

In the last fifty years, attendance at museums in Europe and America has grown significantly, in part as a consequence of mass tourism. Museums have grown in number and in size and our appetite for spectacle and experience, as well as content, has been fed by dramatic new buildings. Frank Gehry's Guggenheim Museum Bilbao established a new model in 1997 and has since stimulated the ambition of small towns and cities across the world.

And yet, as we learn from the essays in this volume, size is rarely important except in the negative. When the writer Orhan Pamuk created his "Museum of Innocence" in Istanbul in 2012, following the publication of his novel of the same name in 2008, he wanted to demonstrate his belief that museums should be modest, of human scale, above all personal. In *The Innocence of Objects*, his manifesto for museums, he wrote:

> big museums with their wide doors call upon us to forget
> our humanity and embrace the state and its human masses.
> … The ordinary everyday stories of individuals are richer,

more humane and much more joyful … It is imperative that museums become smaller, more individualistic and cheaper. This is the only way that they will ever tell stories on a human scale.

Very few of the writers in this anthology embrace the experience of the large or the encyclopaedic museum. This may reflect the circumstances of an invitation to write a short, personal reflection on museums. However, it undoubtedly also discloses a widespread feeling that the most rewarding museum visit is one which involves communion between the viewer and a single object. When I stand in a room before a sculpture made in the fifth century BC, a painting made 500 years ago or a film installation by a living artist, nothing stands between me and the original maker. I feel the form and weight of the object in a shared space, the vibration of colours on the canvas, the sweep of the brush, or the contour of the line on the sheet of paper. These are objects made by another human being, recording his or her perception or sensation of the world, his or her beliefs, transmuted into our own time. It is this intensity, not available through the internet (even though Google's large magnifications of the details of great masterpieces have undoubted allure), that drives us to become a witness to human creation in the museum. The experience of observing and sometimes even holding an object is visceral, haptic and spatial. We situate ourselves in space and in time through the vision of another creative being. Cumulatively, museums offer thousands of small and large epiphanies.

We may also observe that few writers here have chosen to write about the most celebrated museums in large cities. The act of seeking out a distant, small museum can heighten the appetite and the experience in a form of pilgrimage. Small museums are frequently places in which we can withdraw from the pace of everyday life to examine ourselves, or explore the vision of others. They both demand and afford time for reflection and contemplation. In a world dominated by commerce and commodity, by fashion and novelty, museums have become places where values endure. In a society in which a sense of community or common space is now more rare, they provide a location for shared experience. The museum can be a platform for the expression of views and can offer insights into the way in which culture both responds and contributes to changes in society. In the twenty-first century the best museums will create space for conversation, debate and the exchange of ideas, as well as for instruction. Like universities, they can test hypotheses, but they can also attract the kind of broad public that generates a sense of trust and community rare in academic institutions.

It is perhaps surprising that so few of the essays here focus on the experience of the building itself, given the attention paid to museums by leading architects in the nineteenth and in the late twentieth centuries. Alan Hollinghurst's visit to the Thorvaldsensmuseum in Copenhagen is an exception, but in general writers record their relationship with objects rather than with buildings themselves. Nevertheless, as museums become places of congregation as well as places of contemplation, the form of buildings will inevitably evolve. There will be a shift in the balance between space for looking and space for social engagement. In the past 50 years we have already seen significant change through the introduction of classrooms and lecture theatres and later of large shops, restaurants, cafés and "event spaces". In the next 20 years, there will be a demand for rooms in which seminars, debates, conversation and practical work can occur. "Learning" will not be confined to the classroom or the auditorium, but will take place throughout the building, moving us forward from palace to forum: a democratic arena in which we can all learn from each other, from our present and from our past. That said, the unique experience of viewing objects and works of art in close proximity will remain the touchstone of museums. It is this experience which fuels the imagination of so many writers, and it is our privilege to share their insights on the pages that follow.

Nicholas Serota
Director, Tate

Preface

Some people have good ideas in the bath; Tim de Lisle had one of his best in the British Museum. It was the spring of 2008, and he was soon to take over as editor of *The Economist*'s sister magazine, *Intelligent Life*, when he went with his ten-year-old daughter to the BM's Chinese New Year day. The Terracotta Army was sold out, but they amused themselves instead following a trail of lanterns, watching a performance by a Chinese theatre troupe and browsing the stalls in the Great Court, which had been transformed into a giant wok.

That day was to go down in British Museum history as the single best attended they had ever had. Thirty-five thousand visitors passed through the turnstiles, and the main doors had to be shut for the first time since the Chartist riots of 1848.

It struck Tim that a phenomenon like this simply couldn't have happened in his childhood. Back then, in the 1970s, museums were, he remembered, "mostly dreary places: dusty, fusty, impenetrable". He remembered being dragged out by his parents on wet Sunday afternoons to visit the V&A ("frumpy old frocks on headless mannequins"), the Imperial War Museum ("noisy, confusing and tedious") and the Natural History Museum ("one damned skeleton after another").

But in the 30-odd years between his childhood and his children's, the winds of change had blown through museums. They had woken up, become light and welcoming rather than gloomily introverted. The Louvre had sprouted glass pyramids, and the Great Court at the British Museum turned into a glass doughnut.

Inspired by all this, Tim dreamed up a new series. Called "Authors on Museums", its formula was simple, but strong. With each issue of *Intelligent Life* a distinguished writer – not an art critic – would return to a museum that had played some part in their life, and write about what they liked (or didn't) about it, weaving in a thread of memoir.

A couple of years later, I took over the commissioning of the series. I had some interesting misses. Rose Tremain explained that she disliked museums in the same way that she disliked New Year parties – "I feel imprisoned by the demand to come up with a suitable emotional and intellectual response in a very narrow piece of time"; Richard Ford confessed that he gives himself "about 45 minutes before the floors turn to concrete and my eyes don't focus"; David Sedaris admitted that he wasn't a museums kind of person, but "a gift shop and café kind of person".

But more often than not authors were raring to go, and by the time the series drew to a close earlier this year, 38 authors had written about museums that inspired them – even, in some cases, changed their lives. Their choices ranged from the august (John Lanchester on the Prado) to the domestic (Roddy Doyle on the Lower East Side Tenement Museum in New York) and the frankly weird (Aminatta Forna on the Museum of Broken Relationships in Zagreb). What distinguished and unified them all, however, was the quality of writing.

We spent a long time mulling over which pieces to include in this volume, and we think we've chosen 24 of the very best. We hope you enjoy them as much as we have.

Maggie Fergusson

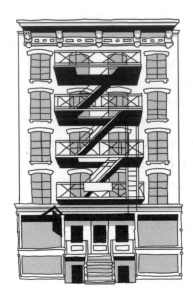

There's Life in These Walls

THE LOWER EAST SIDE TENEMENT MUSEUM, NEW YORK

Roddy Doyle

It is hard to accept that this is a museum. It is hard not to expect a member of the Gumpertz family, probably Mrs Gumpertz, to walk in and demand to know what I'm doing here, in their home.

"Looking at your wallpaper" is the answer.

Mrs Gumpertz – Nathalie, née Rheinsberg – lived here, at 97 Orchard Street, on New York's Lower East Side, a few doors south of Delancey Street. I'm standing in the apartment she occupied with her four children and her husband, Julius, until he left for work one morning in October 1874. He was a shoemaker, a heel cutter, and he never returned.

I live in Dublin, a city of plaques. Renowned writers, revered nation-builders – the city seems to have been full of them. I often wonder what would happen to the architectural glory that is Georgian Dublin if someone unscrewed a plaque. It might collapse. There is a plaque on the front wall of a house across the street from my suburban home: Arthur Griffith, the founder of Sinn Féin, lived there. A ten-minute walk away, there's another – Erwin Schrödinger, physicist and Nobel laureate, lived here between 1939 and 1956. Bram Stoker grew up ten minutes away in the opposite direction, although there's no plaque on the side of that house. Presumably the current occupiers don't want to see their front garden packed, railings to letterbox, with young Japanese vampires. There is a Stoker plaque on the side of a different house, on Kildare Street.

1

I like the plaques. I like knowing that James Joyce lived here, and here, and here and here and here, and that Lord Edward Carson was born over there. I like the surprises – Sheridan Le Fanu lived here, Ernest Shackleton lived here, Ludwig Wittgenstein liked to sit and write at these steps in the winter months of 1948 and 1949. The plaques seem to add depth to the city, to make it at once more Irish and less insular. It is right to celebrate and point out the hard work, the ingenuity, the good luck and bad luck that made these names so famous. But there is the limitation: fame. I have never seen a plaque saying "Mary Collins lived here, 1897–1932; she loved her family", or "Derek Murphy, 1923–2001, printer, sat on these steps and had a smoke on his way home from work. He liked a laugh and always tried his best."

That is why the Tenement Museum is so special and why I'm here for the third time in 15 years. No famous people lived here. But people did.

I'm standing in front of a sewing-machine very like the one that Nathalie Gumpertz must have used to keep her family alive after her husband walked out. We will never know why he left, and that is a big part of the museum's appeal. Each room is assembled – or reassembled – from facts. Birth certificates, census details, court testimonies, pieces of cloth, fragments of wallpaper, corners of linoleum. The rest is left to us. We know he left and we know he never returned. We stand in this room, which has been left – seems to have been left – as it was soon after Nathalie and her children realised that he wasn't coming home. We look at the sewing-machine. It is tiny compared with a modern model. There was no electric light, no gaslight. Four or five strides would get us from one end of the apartment to the door and the narrow, dark hallway outside. Water had to be collected in buckets from the back of the house, down – and back up

– three flights of stairs. Nathalie might have applied for Outdoor Relief, $2 a week, usually in goods – bread, coal – not cash. She might have petitioned her landlord, Lucas Glockner, for help with the rent. She might have been given her sewing-machine by the newly formed United Hebrew Charities. We don't know. The word "tenement" means a building that houses three families or more. Standing in this room gives the word its emotional clout.

But the wallpaper is beautiful. It is a sunny, cold, clear morning but the wallpaper would be beautiful in any weather. It is floral, and gorgeous. I'm not someone who notices wallpaper or furniture. I think that is the first time I have written the word "floral". But this wallpaper is important. It lifts the Gumpertz family – my Gumpertz family – out of misery and sentimentality. It is not the original paper. There are five storeys to this house, and five apartments per floor. In some of the rooms, the people who changed this tenement into a museum found up to 20 layers of wallpaper. They took a fragment of the Gumpertz paper to the company that may have manufactured it in the 1870s, and the company made enough new rolls to cover the parlour walls. But – here is where it's brilliant – the new paper looks as if it's been on the walls for 140 years. The paper looks like an act of defiance: life is dark but the walls are bright and intricate. Nathalie's husband had disappeared and one of their four children, Isaac, died eight months later. The 1870 census lists Nathalie as "keeping house"; by 1880 she's a "dressmaker". The parlour, the front room, has become Nathalie's "shop", where her clients come to place orders for alterations to dresses and jackets. They walk into a bright, cheerful room, into success, hope, faith in the future, faith in the power of a well-stitched garment.

There is one photograph of Nathalie in the room, taken around – or "circa" – 1880. ("Circa" gets used a lot in the Tenement

Museum literature.) She looks tough and careful. She looks like a woman who can make people laugh when she wants to, or needs to.

The tenement at 97 Orchard Street was built in 1863 by Nathalie's landlord, Glockner, a German immigrant, a tailor. At the time, the area now known as the Lower East Side was known as Kleindeutschland – Little Germany. Between that year and 1935, when it was condemned as a residence, at least 7,000 people, immigrants or the children of immigrants, lived there. They came from more than 20 countries.

The museum is all about layers and waves: layers of paint, waves of people. In 1935, the then landlord decided not to make the expensive renovations that new building laws demanded. His tenants couldn't afford the increased rents, so he evicted them and shut the door. The shops on the two lower floors stayed open but the door to the apartments upstairs remained shut – not literally; some of the apartments were used for storage – until 1988, when two women, Ruth Abram, the museum founder, and Anita Jacobson, opened it. I like to think there was a whoosh, then voices, Prussian, Polish, Irish, Italian, speaking in German, Yiddish, Italian, perhaps Gaelic, maybe even English: "What kept you?"

To the visitor, this visitor, Orchard Street is Robert De Niro in *The Godfather: Part II*, using the rooftops on his way to killing Don Fanucci. Keep our eyes above ground level, and we could be looking back 100 years, and more. Standing on the stoop outside the Tenement Museum – even the word "stoop" is exciting: in Ireland we only have steps – I'm looking at a film, hundreds of films, dozens of my favourite scenes.

Inside, in the dark of the narrow hall, I'm brought further back, out of the age of film. (Mind you, it is very like the hall De Niro stood in, his gun wrapped in a blanket, waiting to shoot

Don Fanucci.) It is like looking at a Jacob A. Riis photograph; I'm almost stepping into it. Riis's photographs of the New York tenements and the appalling living standards of the people who lived in them, and his book *How the Other Half Lives* (1890), had forced major housing reforms and improvements. Riis might have stood in this hall. He might have passed through on his way up to photograph and speak to the tenants. It is a bright day outside but the hall is gloomy. (Gas jets were installed in 1905, and electric light in 1924.) It must have been frightening, and dangerous. The wall covering, hung in 1905, perhaps as a response to the installation of the new gaslight, is made of burlap, treated with linseed oil. It is an arresting surface, and attractive, but I can't help seeing a big urchin playing with a box of matches while my babies sleep upstairs.

It is the flaking paint that is strangely moving. This isn't a re-creation. This is the hall as it was; this is the paint. I'm standing where Nathalie Gumpertz passed on her way to fetch water, where, later, Josephine Baldizzi, one of the last tenants, stepped on her way out to school. Their shoulders rubbed these walls; Baldizzi family shoulders brushed against this paint. Prams were parked; buckets of coal and bolts of cloth were carried through. People just off Ellis Island huddled here and wondered what to do.

The life of the house is in the walls, behind the flaking paint, in the flaking paint. It's tempting to rub a hand across a slice of wall, to eliminate the neglect and age, to watch the flakes lift and fall – to cough and laugh. But this hall belongs to the dead and it is actually beautiful, as Havana is beautiful. The question "Why don't they mend it?" is quickly forgotten. The ceiling is pressed metal; the plaster arch, the wooden wainscotting date back to 1863. It is grand and it is also squalid. It is a bit like America must have seemed to the new arrivals.

5

In Ireland the word "landlord" often brings the word "slum" with it, or "absentee". Irish history is all about slum landlords and absentee landlords. I remember, when I was a little boy, holding my father's hand, and looking up at the gaping dark entrance to a Georgian house in Dublin. The glass above the door was broken; the hall behind the open door was dark and huge. Wild kids my own age were running in and out, fighting on the steps. "Why are they there?" I asked my father. "They live there," he told me. The answer frightened me. "Are they bold boys?" I asked. He laughed. "Oh, no," he said. "But they will be."

I know I'm standing in a slum now but there is a painting – a roundel, a medallion – in front of me. There is another one behind me but it is a black smudge. This one has been restored. It is a wooden house, blue sky, bright grass, like the work of a talented child. It is hard to figure out why it is on that particular wall. But it is there and it is bright and, somehow, hopeful. The improvements that Glockner made over the years were demanded by legislation but he must have been proud of this house. It was new once.

Upstairs are rooms that have been left as they were found in 1988. Layers of wallpaper and paint; layers of linoleum. Layers of life. I have often walked through old, neglected houses and imagined making them mine, doing them up and living in them. But there is something precise about the neglect here, even something magical. It is not neglect at all; it is respect. People lived here – people live here.

It is the same further up, in the re-created households, the Gumpertzes' home, and the Rogarshevskys', the Levines', the Moores', the Baldizzis'. The details – a doll, a baby's undershirt, a pair of scissors, a tin of Colman's mustard powder – clutch at us and bring us right up to these people. Strangely, the repeated words "*circa*" and "might" do the same. They calm us down and allow us to move about and feel ourselves at home. The past seems to disappear – the Colman's mustard looks exactly as it docs in my local supermarket. There is very little space but it is used ingeniously. The interior windows – big windows in the inside walls – seem odd, even a bit unsettling. But they work. Daylight gets into the deepest corners. These lives were hard but they were lived in the place where home and cleverness met.

The Baldizzi apartment has something extra, the voice of Josephine, born here in 1926. She left when she was nine, in 1935, when her family was evicted. Her recorded voice fills the rooms. It is a big voice, and very American. Her life here wasn't miserable. "My father could make anything. He had hands of gold." So did the people who decided that this house was to be a museum.

In 1883, nine years after Julius Gumpertz walked out of 97 Orchard Street, Nathalie received notice that her husband had inherited $600, following the death of his father, in Prausnitz, Germany. Julius had to be declared legally dead. Lucas Glockner, her daughter, Rosa, and Nathalie herself signed written testimonies, verifying Julius's disappearance, and Nathalie became the official administrator of his estate. Six hundred dollars was the equivalent of more than four years' rent. She moved, with her three daughters, uptown – further into America – to Yorkville, on the Upper East Side. She could afford to, and the Lower East Side was changing. Many of her new neighbours, like Nathalie, were Jewish. But they were eastern European; they spoke Yiddish. Yorkville was where the Germans were moving to. In 1886, she was living in 237 East 73th Street, and her occupation was "widow". She died eight years later, aged 58, and left her daughters $1,000. They all married within a year of their mother's death.

In 2009, Julius was finally tracked down. He had died in a

Jewish Home for the Aged and Infirm in Cincinnati, Ohio, in 1924. His occupation was "huckster".

The Lower East Side Tenement Museum
103 Orchard Street, New York, NY 10002, United States
www.tenement.org

Rodin's Sonnets in Stone

Allison Pearson

You never forget your first kiss. Mine happened on a school trip to Paris over 30 years ago and it was either a happy coincidence or a divine joke that, during that same Easter, I encountered another unforgettable Kiss. The awkward, though increasingly absorbing, snog with Dave from Oadby on a hummocky camp-bed in a dormitory pungent with teenage socks retains a place in my personal gallery, but no longer in my heart. The other Kiss – by Auguste Rodin – started a love affair with a small museum on the Left Bank in which *Le Baiser* sits among the sculptor's sublime works and several fine pieces by his mistress, Camille Claudel. The kisses bestowed by art, unlike those of men, are set in stone.

It was in the Musée Rodin that I first realised what Art was capable of. Trailing along behind Monsieur S., our strenuously Francophile teacher in his sadly unironic beret, we had already "done" Notre Dame. Then came a route march through the Louvre. Before its airy makeover with the glass pyramid, the Louvre felt like the worst kind of museum: punishingly vast, the walls of its interminable corridors lined with dukes with beards like spades and spoilt, mean-mouthed women in poodle wigs. After some hours, footsore and deafened by culture, we got to the Mona Lisa. I remember thinking how small she was. And how podgy. The famous smile hinted at embarrassment that all these people would bother coming so far to see her, when really she

11

was nothing special. We adored Monsieur S. and we listened to him hold forth, complete with faux-Gallic gesticulations, about a turning point in the history of portraiture, the subtle handling of flesh tones, blah blah. But it was no good. The *Mona Lisa* was such a masterpiece, we could hardly see her. Or discover her secret for ourselves, as teenagers badly need to do, whether in love or art.

The last thing we wanted at the end of that day was another damned museum. But with the light fading to the freckled silver that makes the Parisian skyline look like an early photographic print, we found ourselves in rue de Varenne. You have to cross a cobbled yard to get to the front door of the Hôtel Biron. The Biron is actually a perfect small chateau, like a doll's house lowered from heaven into seven acres of exquisite formal gardens in Faubourg Saint-Germain. Built *circa* 1730, it was first a private house, then a school. By 1905 it was in disrepair and the rooms were let out to several tenants. At one point, they included Jean Cocteau, Henri Matisse, Isadora Duncan, the poet Rainer Maria Rilke and Rodin himself. The queue for the bathroom must have been quite something.

In 1916, when Rodin was 75, it was agreed that the building would become the Rodin Museum, and he donated his own collection, along with all of his sculptures and the lesser-known drawings, with their clean-lined foreshadowings of Matisse's *Odalisques.*

Although Rodin died before it opened in 1919, it's hard to think of another museum where the presence of its creator can be felt so strongly. Frankly, it would be a disappointment if, after hours, a heavily bearded figure did not come down the curving marble staircase like Moses in his nightshirt and continue the mighty work of freeing his figures from their marble prisons. Let my people go.

All great artists are self-plunderers. After they've gone through the phase of stealing from their heroes, they begin to raid their own work. It's not a question of running out of ideas or cynically recycling, rather an impulse born of the fanatical conviction that this time, just like the Michelin-starred chef Joël Robuchon in his restaurant near by, you are going to get the balance of ingredients exactly right, and conjure from them something that even you may not have foreseen. Nowhere does one glimpse that remorseless reworking as clearly as in these tall, elegant salons.

Just ahead, when you walk through the main door, with the Cinderella staircase on your right, is *Walking Man* (1900–1907), a giant, headless bronze figure. *Walking Man* was assembled from two legs originally created for *St John the Baptist Preaching* and from a fragment of another torso that Rodin had lying around. Over by the windows, the light streaming in from the garden bestows a holy radiance on a pair of hands called *The Secret*. Reproduced almost as often as Dürer's drawing of hands at prayer, these barely touching fingers have been lauded for their verisimilitude. Look more closely, however, and you see that the sculptor has pressed two right hands together. Auguste Rodin was never going to allow any work of his to be all fingers and thumbs. If the left hand is spoiling your perfect symmetry, then ditch it and use the other hand twice.

No less unashamed, and even more thought-provoking, is the twist that Rodin gave to *The Martyr*. This sprawled figure, head thrown back, one arm flung wide as if to catch herself, was from the start forged in ambiguity. To what, exactly, is she being martyred: to private bedroom ecstasy or public pain? She doesn't know whether she's coming or going to heaven. You find her – as you do, in embryo, so many of Rodin's signature forms (including

The Thinker, The Falling Man, Fugit Amor and *The Prodigal Son*) – in *The Gates of Hell*, the vast doors commissioned by the French state in 1880 and left uncompleted on Rodin's death in 1917.

The Gates now dominate a wall in the gardens, nearest to the road. I have never liked them, much preferring the doors of the Baptistry in Florence that were Rodin's inspiration but which, with their strict geometry, make better visual sense of the mêlée. His gateway is almost too much to take in, not just at first glance but after long contemplation: a vertical battlefield, writhing with bodies caught between life and death. (How it would have struck anyone returning from the western front we can barely imagine.) But Rodin lifted his *Martyr* from her wall, and gave her a solo performance. Then, in 1896, he flipped her over, strapped a pair of wings to her back, and arranged for her to plummet into her marble plinth, nose to the ground. This time she was labelled "Illusion: Icarus's Sister", which is pushing it a bit. We all know about the waxy boy and his reckless brush with the sun, but who knew that falling ran in the family?

(Over the years, my suspicions have grown about Rodin's use of mythological titles. The hotter the sex, the more it is graced – and thus excused, for cultivated viewers of his time – by a classical tag. *Psyche, Transported to Heaven*, says the label on a turn-of-the-century drawing, but whether Psyche was really in transport, or just enjoying having that very pretty boy blow on her right nipple, is hard to determine.)

All of these art-historical layers are fascinating, and they offer a masterclass in creativity, but not one bit of them struck me back in 1975. I was too busy being amazed. For the first-timer, Musée Rodin delivers a two-fisted shock. The space itself, though grand, is intimate and all the lovelier for being scuffed and peeling; within the formal restraint of its two floors are contained – but barely contained – lust and dejection and jealousy and violence and love, both orgasmically requited and for ever out of reach. Look at *L'Eternelle Idole*, with the naked man kneeling in front of a naked woman who is raised slightly above him and deigning to glance down as the poor fellow plants a kiss just below her breasts. Does she seem to pity him? Do his arms, crossed awkwardly behind his back rather than wrapped around the girl, suggest he is less her lover and more a helpless supplicant, a slave to a passion from which there is no escape? And then there is *The Kiss* itself.

Three decades on, I wonder what I saw in this monumental snog. It would sit perfectly in a Las Vegas chapel of lurve. Sometimes marble feels too smooth, too chilly for Rodin's purposes; these days, I am moved by the rougher and readier terracotta *Kiss* that sits in a modest glass case to one side of the original. Still, I owe that first *Kiss*. For a group of weary teenagers from the Midlands, here was remarkable news. Dead people had felt these things; and the living went on feeling them. Rodin's sculptures made that connection for us; they continued to struggle and gasp and yearn and caress beneath their marmoreal skins.

Four years later, I was an undergraduate sitting in the Cambridge Arts Cinema watching Roberto Rossellini's *Journey to Italy*, with Ingrid Bergman and George Sanders as a desperately unhappy couple who visit the archaeological museum at Pompeii.

Looking at the casts of the agonised figures trapped in ash, Bergman is overcome. I recognised the expression on her face. She sees with devastating clarity that she and her husband are not the first to have suffered so, nor will they be the last. What Vesuvius did by accident, Rodin did by design.

I wouldn't recommend the Musée Rodin to anyone in an ailing marriage. The imperative to seize what happiness you can is so overwhelming that a divorce lawyer would do a roaring trade if he set up a stall by the exit. The museum has become a place of romantic rendezvous. On my latest visit, I was with the father of my children. We had come to Paris for a weekend, as so many middle-aged couples do, to see if we could pick up the traces of the lovers now known as Mummy and Daddy. I was shocked when he mentioned casually that, many years before, these gardens had been the location of a tryst of his own. "But it's my museum," I protested. An idiotic thing to say but, when we find a place we love, we are torn between wanting to share it with the world and hug it to ourselves. The Rodin still feels like my secret, but it turns out to be an open one, as it should be.

This time, we headed straight for the quieter rooms upstairs. (The impulse to touch the marble flesh can be overwhelming and, in my experience, the attendants up there are more likely to turn a blind eye than the "Défense de Toucher" enforcers down below; but please don't quote me.) Some of the place's greatest pleasures are not the most obvious. Like Edward Steichen's majestic photograph of Rodin's *Balzac* at dusk. The collection holds more than 8,000 images of the artist and his work: snapshots of time-travel, allowing us to see how others saw him in his day. In my favourite, a Rodin grizzled with age is getting to grips with a giant plaster cast of *The Hand of God*. The maker meets his Maker, and his match.

On what must be my seventh visit, I walk without hesitation to *La Danaïde*. Face down with her long hair streaming in front of her, the young woman is condemned to pour water forever into a bottomless vase. Still, by compensation, Rodin has given her what may be the most gorgeous back in all art. Any woman would die for such eloquent alabaster shoulder blades. She should be introduced to Michelangelo's *David*: they would produce the most beautiful stone babies.

On the last night of that school trip, Monsieur S., my one really good teacher, called me into his room and with those frantic, faux-Gallic hands backed me into a cupboard and tried to undo my blouse. Even at that young age, I felt pity rather than disgust or fear. This too was to be part of my education. But not a part that would have shocked Rodin, who knew all about the thousand natural shocks that flesh is heir to, aggressive as well as tender.

If you walk to the bottom of the gardens down the gravel path and turn and look past the fountain to the Hôtel Biron, you have no idea how many chunks of human nature that beautiful storehouse contains. I first went there as a young girl, knowing nothing, and I hope to be there as a wise old woman, marvelling at feelings that once were mine. *The Kiss* may be just a kiss, but the fundamental things apply. As time goes by.

Musée Rodin
79 Rue de Varenne, 75007 Paris, France
www.musee-rodin.fr/

Cool Under Fire

Rory Stewart

Two vast and mostly trunkless legs of stone stand in the hall; near them sits a shattered Bodhisattva with hunched shoulders and sorrowful gaze – the work of an Afghan sculptor 1,700 years ago. In 2001, the Taliban broke it into a hundred pieces. And the Bodhisattva seems to be mourning all the cracks and plaster joints of its reconstruction.

It is difficult not to write about the Kabul Museum as a lament, and perhaps that was true long before the Taliban. The single white marble door on your left as you enter probably comes from the Kabul bazaar, burnt by the British in 1842 in revenge for their humiliation in the first Anglo-Afghan war, or from the Royal Palace in the Bala Hissar, destroyed in 1880 during the second British occupation. The museum bears the scars of the rocket that hit it in the spring of 1993, and of the militias who broke into the storeroom the following autumn, ransacking the cases, burning the records and removing most of the collection.

And yet it is not a depressing place. I first saw it at the beginning of 2002. I had walked from Herat to Kabul that winter. I had seen hundreds of pickaxe-wielding villagers, directed by Pakistani traders, uncovering, looting and destroying the ancient city of the Turquoise Mountain, the lost Afghan capital of the Middle Ages. The Taliban had just blown up two monumental Buddhas that had stood, carved into the side of a cliff in the Bamiyan Valley, since the sixth century. I found new craters, left by looters, on mountain ridges at 11,000 feet. In this country of isolated hamlets, the life expectancy was 37, literacy rates in the south were 8 per cent and archaeological looting had become a common occupation, along with heroin production and mercenary fighting.

Central Kabul seemed like one extended security checkpoint. You were stopped by men who ripped car doors open and pointed their rifles at passengers. You found roads narrowing suddenly into tunnels of sandbags, or closed altogether by concrete blast walls. You were pushed off the street by armoured vehicles with blaring sirens, by embassy convoys, by militias in pick-up trucks.

But the wide, 5-mile boulevard leading south-west to the Kabul Museum took one back into a more peaceful nation. You could see the snow peaks on either side. Men, oblivious to the traffic, sat back on empty carts, pulled by ambling donkeys. This had been the first paved road in the country. King Amanullah had driven his seven Rolls-Royces down it in the 1920s, and although, since then, the avenue of plane trees had been cut for firewood, it was still paved. At the end of the boulevard, framed by 15,000-foot peaks and facing the museum, was his great ruined palace of Darul Aman – "the place of peace".

The museum was not surrounded, like a NATO base, with razor wire and blast walls. Nor was it one of the garish palaces of the new Afghan rich, with bulging filigree balconies and pink cupolas. Nor, again, was it covered with the green tiles favoured by drug barons and warlords, contractors and ministers. Instead, here was a two-storey 1930s villa, with walls of muted grey pebbledash and a small line of white plaster decoration beneath the roof. Outside it in a shed stood two 1950s American cars, partially concealed by brown canvas sheets. And a railway engine, for a railway that does not exist.

The entrance remained unchanged since the piratical Hungarian archaeologist Sir Aurel Stein visited in 1943. (He died in Kabul at the age of 80 and is buried in the British cemetery.) The glass of the ticket booth was plastered with fading postcards. In the tattered pile behind the desk were brochures produced during the Soviet occupation of the 1980s, or President Daud's regime in the 1970s, or even under the old monarchy. And the two ladies sitting in the booth seemed to have been there through all those years, always in half-darkness, finishing their lunch, surprised to be asked for a ticket.

Since that first visit, $300 billion has been spent on Afghanistan by the international community, but nothing has changed in the museum. The ladies are still finishing their lunch. The pieces on the first floor and the landing do not seem so much displayed as left in situ, as though exposed in some archaeological site. There are none of the tricks of the modern curator. You do not enter a hushed dark hall, with a few treasures picked out in muted lighting. There are no hidden spotlights, encouraging you to see each piece as a symbol of the mystery and the wisdom of the ancients. The exhibits stand, in full daylight, in a small, white-walled hall. The headless statue of Kanishka, in his vast felt boots and pleated trousers, has been smashed, repaired and placed back in almost exactly the same position in which he stood in 1976. There are no artfully chosen colour schemes, no old quotations or illustrated maps, no provocative juxtapositions, interpretative panels, audio-guides or glossy catalogues. Often, there are no signs at all. And there are rarely any visitors.

The foreign diplomats, NGO workers and 10,000 consultants in Kabul are paid by employers who insist on bodyguards for most trips and view cultural visits as an unnecessary indulgence. And while, elsewhere in the city, Afghans are enjoying the return of culture – a reading of Rumi's poetry can fill a garden with silent men and women cross-legged on carpets, and Sufi music attracts huge crowds – they are only slowly beginning to value and visit their museum.

Only one piece on the ground floor – the Bodhisattva – is in a glass case. The others do not seem so much art as hefted facts. The half-chipped mihrab seems to trail plaster dust. The basin in the front hall is also dusty; but nothing can subdue the gleam of the cold black marble. It is nearly 8 feet in circumference, carved with lotus blossoms below, suggesting that it was once a Buddhist basin, and a fading Kufic inscription above, recording its re-use in a medieval seminary in Kandahar.

You can smell the cedar of the old statues from the pagan culture of north-eastern Afghanistan on the first-floor landing. At the end of the long room, dimly lit through faded, dusty curtains, is a figure with skinny legs, a flat face and a perfunctory attempt at a sword, astride a crude, simplified horse. The deodar tree from which he was carved must have been 9 feet in diameter, and perhaps preceded the arrival of Islam, not just in Nuristan but in South Asia.

Most of these hero statues were destroyed when Nuristan was conquered and forcibly converted to Islam in the 1890s. A hundred years later, they were smashed by the mujahideen (including groups in the current government), and then repaired. Then smashed again by the Taliban, and again repaired. But what you notice is the roughness not of the iconoclasts, but of the sculptors. Most pieces bear the brutal marks of the rough adze. Only the great ball of the mounted figure's stomach is smooth.

But the revelation when I visited in the spring was the new exhibition on the second floor. Here foreign curators have worked with the Afghan staff to paint the walls a subdued red, and to introduce glass cases displaying a series of small sculptures only recently excavated. Here, too, is carving in ancient aromatic cedar, but there are no marks of adze or chisel, and no comical proportions. They remind us that almost 2,000 years before the Nuristani statues were carved, Afghan craftsmen were producing Buddhas in wood and stone, in bronze and terracotta and gold leaf: delicate, naturalistic pieces, perfectly finished, whose serene human faces changed Asian art for ever. And gathered together they shift our whole perception of second-century Afghanistan.

They come from the time of the Yue-chih dynasty, which can often seem the epitome of barbarian vulgarity. These steppe horsemen crushed the last surviving successors of Alexander the Great, overthrew the Greek theatres and left the inscription from the oracle of Delphi in ruins. Even their attempts at civilisation, finance, faith and art can seem farcical. On their coinage, fine Macedonian heads are replaced by cartoon figures in baggy boots, and the script is a nonsense of back-to-front Greek letters, etched by illiterates. The coins display 50 different deities from Hercules to Shiva's bull, Nandi, with little sign of theological discrimination. And the fine treasures found near their palace at Begram are imports – Chinese lacquer, glass from Alexandria, sinuous ivories of dancing maidens from India – which may simply have been heaped in a storehouse on the trade route.

But in this small, second-floor room, the supposedly barbarian kingdom stands revealed as one of the great, and most puzzling, of the ancient civilisations. The pieces are from Mes Aynak, 25 miles south-east of Kabul, where archaeologists have just uncovered a complex of second-century Buddhist religious sites with an astonishing depth of faith and artistry. The figures at the base of these Indian-featured Buddhas wear Macedonian skirts and Persian beards. The gold leaf has fallen off the nose of the figure in the corner, but his heavy-lidded gaze is intact and his serenity still challenges the unbeliever. The sandstone Buddha leans towards you, hand turning in energetic benediction. This is Buddhism with a very distinct and dignified Afghan form. Where else in the world does one see such solid standing Buddhas, legs firmly planted on broad toes, with the sharp waves of draperies in movement? Where else would one find a naked man beside the Buddha? Or a seated Bodhisattva in black schist with a wrinkled lip and a free nomad's swagger?

These pieces, found among 1,000 acres of monasteries and stupas between Himalayan peaks, are hundreds of years older than the Buddhism of Tibet. They are among the very first human depictions of the Buddha, and belong to the early crest of a great missionary Buddhism that was eventually to push west to Iran and north through Central Asia to Japan. Archaeologists working at the site have found a stupa 50 feet high, a 20-foot Buddha, half-buried in the earth, and a reclining Buddha so vast that it fills an image hall. There are fragments of frescoes, gold and lapis-lazuli blue, on the earth walls of the monasteries. And they are under threat not from the Taliban but from the international community. The Chinese government, with international support, will soon bulldoze and dynamite the entire site of Mes Aynak to create a copper mine. The French archaeological delegation is working with Afghans to try to salvage what they can before the site becomes a crater.

But as Mes Aynak disappears, the Kabul Museum will, I believe, survive. It endures ultimately because it is a deeply Afghan institution. The director, Dr Omar Khan Masudi, has been in place, in his pinstriped suit, since 1978. He did not leave during the civil war, when an Afghan antiquity could sell for over $100,000 in Peshawar. He was one of the few who knew where the Bactrian Treasure, the extraordinary hoard of gold ornaments discovered in northern Afghanistan shortly before the Soviet invasion, had been hidden; and he kept the secret for nine years when many thought it had been stolen. Since the American-led invasion, he has resisted new temptations: the chance to be outside the country for much of the year accompanying travelling exhibitions to Europe, or to take up a fellowship at an Ivy League university. And he patiently absorbs the blandishments, arrogance and bewilderment of the international agencies, pressing to transform Afghanistan and the museum with it. I have seen him in San Francisco and London, but somehow, whenever I return to Kabul, there he is, moving slowly through the halls of the museum.

Over green tea and walnuts in his office, I ask Masudi what he thinks about the imminent destruction of Mes Aynak. He looks back at me through his tinted glasses and refuses to be drawn. It has been ordained that Afghanistan needs foreign currency, and that the copper mine is the answer. Foreigners who would not contemplate dynamiting Westminster Abbey for a lithium store, or the Parthenon for tin, feel that destroying the last remains of one of the great lost civilisations is justifiable if it produces income for the Afghan exchequer. This is, after all, only Afghanistan: what does it matter? But the Kabul Museum, with its empty galleries, its quiet displays and its loyal staff, stands as a reminder of older values, of an attitude to the past that we too once shared.

The National Museum of Afghanistan
Darulaman Road, Kabul, Afghanistan
www.nationalmuseum.af/

Cabinets of Wonder

PITT RIVERS MUSEUM, OXFORD

Frank Cottrell-Boyce

When you approach the desk at the Pitt Rivers, the question they are expecting is, "Where are the shrunken heads?" The heads are the star exhibits – they inspired a scene in Harry Potter! – but the museum is sensitive about them. When we wanted to take pictures for this article, they said, "Of course, anything you like, except the heads." After all, they are human remains. They deserve respect. So, with respect, we have no photographs, only my description.

The ground floor of the Pitt Rivers is an enchanting, crepuscular clutter. The display cases have titles such as Puppets, Instruments of Divination, Lamellophones (surprisingly numerous and widespread) and – the one you're looking for – Treatment of Dead Enemies. It could be an aquarium designed by Hieronymus Bosch. A dozen shrunken heads float fishily from wires. One has a mop of black hair like a bio-engineered Beatles souvenir, another a carrying handle thrust through its nose, like a fashion accessory from Mordor. Their faces are full of character. There's no doubt that family and friends would recognise them.

Most of the heads were made by the peoples of Ecuador and Peru. Until the 1960s Shuar men fought a running war with the Achuar, taking heads and turning them into tsantsas. These aren't really trophies. Making tsantsas was a kind of post-mortem adoption process whereby the soul of a dead enemy becomes part of his conqueror's family. Once a tsantsa was complete, the shrunken head had no value: it had done its job. So Shuar and Achuar warriors were quite happy to trade them, which is how they ended up here. The heads were so popular that people took to making and trading fakes. The one donated by Pitt-Rivers himself is made of a sloth's head. Others were made from the heads of poor people stolen from mortuaries. We know this because they are stuffed, not with rainforest vegetation, but with a copy of the *Quito Times*.

The presence of the heads raises questions about what a great ethnographic collection is really for. Does this cabinet of day-to-day wonders help us to understand other cultures better, to uncover our common humanity? Or does it titillate our sense of superiority to the exotic "others" who made them? It was definitely the promise of the exotic that first brought me here. I was a student in Oxford in the early 1980s. When I wanted to impress a girl, I offered to take her to see the shrunken heads. Although I would then demonstrate my more sensitive side by pointing out the interlocking chi balls – 11 filigree ivory spheres, delicate as lace, one inside the other, all carved from a single piece of ivory. A miracle. No wonder she married me. But then the whole of Oxford seemed exotic to me then. I spent my first year in a kind of belligerent daze. I couldn't believe that: (a) it was all so beautiful; and (b) I was allowed to wander round it. I sought out arcane routes across town, crossing obscure quadrangles, cutting through hidden cloisters, going to libraries and faculty buildings not my own, pushing deeper into the labyrinth and pushing my luck – waiting for someone to challenge my right to be there. That's how I found my way to the little door at the back of the Natural History Museum that leads to the Pitt Rivers.

Nowadays it's well signposted and staffed. Back then it took a bit of nerve to step out of the soaring daylight of the Natural History Museum into the shadows of the Pitt Rivers. A museum hidden, tucked inside a museum. Inside there were more doors to dare. The cabinets had drawers: was I allowed to open them? In the corner was a glass case covered with a curtain. I pulled the curtain aside and found a vast red and yellow cloak, an 'ahu 'ula made in the 1830s for Queen Kekauluoki of Lahina in Hawaii, of hundreds of thousands of tiny red and yellow honeysucker feathers. These were supplied by specialists who plucked a few from each bird before letting it go. Each feather is tied into place. The priceless finished 'ahu 'ula was one of the last to be made. The species of honeysucker from which the feathers were taken is now extinct.

Like an ivory ball inside another ivory ball, each exhibit is wrapped inside a sequence of stories. First the story of how it was made. There's the policeman's amulet made from an old coin and a piece of rope from the neck of Campi, a robber hanged for murder in Paris in 1883. Having been shriven for his execution, Campi was in a state of grace, so his relics might have curative powers. The great Haida totem pole was commissioned by Chief Aniithlas to celebrate the adoption of a daughter. I think of the little girl standing outside the chief's "Star House" with the lowering history of her new family staring down at her through the eyes of cedarwood ravens, bears and beavers.

Then there are the stories of how these things got here. Sometimes the labels give poignant hints. The Fijian necklace of sperm-whale teeth, given to the Revd Calvert around 1874, was donated years later by his granddaughter in memory of her son, Pilot Officer James Lionel Calvert, who died on active service in 1939. The beautiful Benin plaques were acquired as a result of the punitive British expedition of 1897 in which Benin City was razed to the ground, its art treasures stolen and auctioned off to offset the costs incurred by the destruction.

Twenty thousand of the objects were donated by Pitt-Rivers himself. He was born Augustus Lane-Fox, in 1827, but changed his name in accordance with the terms of an unexpected and colossal inheritance that transformed him from an officer in the Grenadiers into a collector on an historic scale. Hidden in the heart of every museum is one invisible but crucial exhibit: the original Idea that brought the objects together. These Ideas are often more strange and antiquated than the objects themselves. Pitt-Rivers's Idea was unusually complex. Despite the plaques and the shrunken heads, he was drawn not to plunder and treasure but to the mundane. Most collections in the 19th century told stories of race and nationality: Egyptians and Greeks, Romans and Vikings etc. Pitt-Rivers organised his thematically: money, weapons, saddles, hunting and so on. Those shrunken heads sit alongside the heart of an Irish warrior that was (literally) salted away inside a heart-shaped lead casket, a helmet from the Great War and images of Cromwell's head on a pike. European tarot cards share a space with Congolese divination bones, Yorkshire funeral biscuits with Chinese burial headdresses.

Pitt-Rivers was no early cultural relativist. He was an enthusiastic Darwinian. Certain over-enthusiastic Christians get too literal; over-enthusiastic Darwinians tend to be too metaphorical –taking the literal truth of evolution and applying it to culture. Pitt-Rivers arranged his objects into "types". He proposed a science of "typology" that showed how day-to-day objects evolved like species. Of course they evolved faster in some places than others. "Typology", he wrote, "forms a tree of progress, and distinguishes the leading shoots from the minor branches. The problems of the naturalist and those of the typologist are analogous."

He was less concerned with proving the superiority of the West than with proving that real progress was slow and thus violent political change was against the laws of nature. His typological sequences are sentences pleading for reform over revolution.

Today these sentences are inaudible, and the collection sings a different song. The overwhelming impression it leaves is that no matter where we fetch up – on a shingle strand in the Arctic or a patch of rainforest – we are driven to create. We need to make things beautiful almost as much as we need to make them edible. There are amazing coats made of seal-intestine from remotest Alaska. There are rattles made of puffin beaks from North America – in the desert and on the ice we want to make music. There is a lamp made from a recycled light bulb from Chitungwiza township in Zimbabwe. But the most moving object in the whole museum is in a case acquired from the Masindi District refugee camp in Uganda in 1998: an empty insecticide tin, reshaped with wires and a plastic nozzle to make a toy, an elegant yellow aeroplane. Even in the most wretched circumstances, we dream of flight, and we share that dream with our children.

Pitt Rivers Museum
South Parks Road, Oxford, United Kingdom
www.prm.ox.ac.uk

Painting in Stone

MUSEO DELL'OPIFICIO DELLE PIETRE DURE, FLORENCE

Margaret Drabble

I first saw Florence aged 17, and it changed the colours of the visible world for ever. I came from a country of green and grey, from a sober Quaker schooling in York, where the incomprehensibly Gothic Minster rose in flights of serious masonry into a sombre English sky. Florence was bright and luminous and light of heart, and its churches were polychrome. This astonished me, as we had never studied architecture. I had never seen anything like those façades, their delicate pinks and whites and greens and greys, their stripes and bands and barley-sugar twists of marble, their cloisters of cypresses and orange trees. I had crossed the Alps, alone in a second-class sleeper, and come out of a dark tunnel into a paradise of sunlit colour. I had stumbled, like a time traveller, into the Renaissance.

I have since found that Florence too has its sombre aspect, and some of its streets are dark steep-sided ravines. The Via degli Alfani, which houses one of its most interesting and little-known museums, is austere, with tall, barred and shuttered buildings, rubbish bins, scaffolding and graffiti, and little shops selling electrical parts and polychrome ice creams. If you walk up the Via dei Servi from the Duomo towards the Piazza SS. Annunziata, where the bronze Giambologna statue of Ferdinand I de' Medici stares at you from his horse, you cross the narrow Via degli Alfani and see to your left the limp flags of Italy and the European Union, dangling darkly from an upper storey. They mark the dour façade of the Museo dell'Opificio delle Pietre Dure, the Museum of Semi-Precious Stones, now home to the Medici workshop founded by Duke Ferdinand in 1588. You may also see long queues snaking along the pavement to see Michelangelo's *David* in the nearby Accademia, but you need not stand in line for the treasure house of the Opificio. You can wander through it with a sense of private privilege rare in this overcrowded city.

Many a sightseer is bewitched by the enchanting gold and silverwork of the Ponte Vecchio and the shockingly desirable handbags in the boutiques and the markets. An impulse towards pattern and decoration and inlay is embedded in the Florentine spirit, flourishing in tiny miniatures and vast marble floors, in paintings and textiles and altarpieces. The art of "stone painting" is a curious form of this impulse, and its history is well displayed and documented in the museum. A stroll round the ground floor dazzles you with magnificent purple and black marble table tops from the 18th and 19th centuries, decorated with semi-precious flowers and butterflies, with musical instruments, with birds of exotic plumage, with shells and fishes, with strings of pearls so realistic that it is hard to believe you cannot hang them around your throat. The colours have great subtlety and purity – the blue of a ribbon or a blossom, the intense and living red of a coral or a pomegranate, the soft grey-purple bloom of a plum, the speckled yellow-brown of a ripe pear so tender that you want to sink your teeth into it – and yet fashioned, miraculously, of flat smooth polished stone.

It is easy to see why the first Grand Dukes of Tuscany favoured the opulence of artefacts that signified wealth, status and endurance. Lorenzo de' Medici (1449–92), known as Lorenzo the Magnificent, loved the red Egyptian porphyry, with its claims of royal grandeur and imperial power. His learned and eccentric descendant Francesco, brother of Ferdinand the workshop's founder, preferred the brightness and intricate cut of semi-precious stones. Renaissance science endowed these gems with alchemical and semi-magical properties, but the workshop also looked back to antique models, newly rediscovered. The workshop specialised in a Florentine development of the old Roman technique known as *opus sectile*, a form of mosaic composed not of thousands of individual identical small tesserae, but of pieces of marble, tile or stone pre-cut into shapes and then assembled into geometric or figural patterns like a giant jigsaw. These elaborate hard-stone designs were used for many decorative purposes: to adorn cabinets, to create table tops, chess boards, jewel boxes, caskets and to serve as wall paintings. They embodied a love of the antique wedded to a desire for rich pattern, realistic representation and a perfect mimicry of nature.

The craftsmanship is superb. In the finest pieces it is impossible to see the joins, and in the restoration workshop behind the museum students are still learning to create a perfect illusion. Trompe l'oeil is delightful, yet also perplexing. The mystery deepens the more one gazes into the heart of the stone. Why should this transformation be so compelling? Why do we stare in such wonder at a slice of agate that looks just like a cloudy sky or a flowing river or a girl's cheek? And which do we find more pleasing, the illusory softness of the peach or pear, or the geometry of the pomegranate? Hard-stone designers love pomegranates – nature's own mosaics, with those glinting red seeds begging to be turned to stone.

Clarice Innocenti, the director of the museum, said that to display their skill artists would set themselves the hardest tasks – she used the word *sfida*, or "challenge". In the 18th century the vogue for picturesque landscapes produced some delicate *pietre dure* paintings, such as the museum's small and finely toned view of the Pantheon in Rome, rendered in chalcedony and petrified stone. The museum also has a version of the famous view of the tomb of Cecilia Metella on the Appian Way, beloved by Goethe (another version is in the Gilbert Collection at the V&A). This was a subject proposed by the master goldsmith Louis Siries to Ferdinand III of Lorraine to adorn the vastnesses of the Palazzo Pitti: architecture, he argued, "is the subject that can be represented most perfectly" in hard stone. Add some peasants, two cows and a goat, and you have a pleasingly rustic image of antiquity overlaid by layers of time and a picturesque sensibility.

Painting in stone embodies what W. B. Yeats described as "the fascination of what's difficult". The Opificio has its own school, the Scuola di Alta Formazione, and in the workshop I met two of its star graduates, a dedicated young mosaicist called Sara Guarducci and an eager goldsmith, Paolo Belluzzo. They showed me what the technique of cutting and assembling the stone sections involved. They are artists, keeping ancient crafts alive, and Sara proudly displayed the pieces she was restoring or creating. You can't afford to make mistakes with expensive materials such as lapis lazuli, agate, chalcedony and jasper. (Marble is softer and easier to work.) Sara, dark-haired and white-coated, used a fretsaw made of a wooden chestnut bow strung with a thin wire, and cut into a thin slice of stone mounted on a vice. Using an abrasive paste, she sawed round the edges of a small stencilled shape (a petal? a foot? a cloud?) to create a stone shape that would in the fullness of time become part of an assembled image, a finished jigsaw. This is exactly how the earliest wooden jigsaw pieces were cut, from thin slices of mahogany, in the 18th century.

The workshop also restores Roman mosaics and Renaissance statues in an atmosphere of scholarly expertise. Shattered and scattered antiquities find their way there to be painstakingly reassembled. The work in hand included a statue by Michelangelo belonging to the Duke of Seville, blown to pieces in the Spanish civil war, and a mosaic Roman fountain with nereids. In the courtyard lie unpromising chunks of rock in cages, dull, knobbly hidden gems, waiting their turn to be sawn. The machine that polishes them is not unlike a salami slicer. It grips a lump of mineral and slowly reveals a beauty never before seen by a human eye.

Returning to the museum, I explored the upper gallery, where you can see venerable wooden machines like the ones Sara Guarducci still operates. There were showcases and cabinets full of mineral specimens in an astonishing range of hues, with formations that suggest mountain ranges, oceans, foliage, towers and palaces, even skyscrapers. Jasper, chalcedony, fire-marble with fossil shells, mother-of-pearl, travertine, cipollino – the very names are poetry. There are agates from Volterra and Goa and Sardinia, granites from Egypt and England, lapis lazuli from Persia and Siberia. From Florence's river, the Arno, comes a strangely suggestive marbled river-stone, *pietra paesina*, especially useful in landscapes such as the one showing Dante and Virgil in the Inferno.

The selection of the stone is the all-important moment in the translation of a design, and it explains why the final products are so much livelier and more life-like than the painted originals. Dr Innocenti, kindly taking me on a somewhat breathless tour as she was expecting a television crew, was eloquent about this difference, and the new official guidebook (an improvement on the quaint version I bought years ago) puts it well: "Colours which seemed carefully controlled with a brush were actually the fruit of nature's fantasy; supple drawing and soft shapes were actually obtained by the makers' arduous care with the hard material ..."

It is this act of transformatory magic that brings me back here. The stones, when fashioned by the Medici craftsmen, become something other than themselves and give us a glimpse into the early days of our universe when the inorganic thrust itself towards the organic, bursting into a glorious diversity of fiery forms.

The museum tells a story of decline in the 19th century, when the market for expensive items faltered under the pressures of a strife-torn Italy. Elaborate pieces from the workshop remained unsold, to find their final resting place here. There is a poignancy about the abandoned works on show amid the artificial flowers of the final room. They capture the end of an era, symbolised by a black marble table on which an absent-minded lady returning from a party appears to have dropped a white camellia, a necklace and a ring, a frozen moment which now has a casual permanence.

Out in Florence's older gift shops, you can still find little wall-plaque reproductions of hard-stone paintings, which may even have been hand-crafted, as they claim, in Italy. They are not cheap. A copy of the finely dressed woman in orange and yellow who adorns the Opificio guidebook is on sale for €900. The post-cards are a much better bargain, and I stocked up with scenes from Ariosto, childlike 17th-century peasant landscapes, shells and periwinkles and parrots. The images reproduce beautifully. A yellow hard-stone rose on a postcard is treasure enough for me.

Museo dell'Opificio delle Pietre Dure
Via degli Alfani 78, Florence, Italy
www.opificiodellepietredure.it

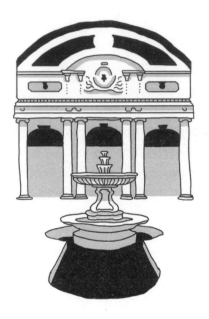

Sanctum in the City

THE FRICK COLLECTION, NEW YORK

Don Paterson

New York has shaped most of my major life choices. My first serious adult relationship was with a New Yorker; my closest friend was a New Yorker; my partner is a New Yorker. I may never be one, but if "home" is where one relaxes most, the length of my exhalation when I fall out of Penn Station seems to indicate something beyond mere relief.

It's not too mysterious. First, there's the way the natives communicate: they speak the way I prefer to be spoken to – nice and quickly, with an overdeveloped sense of irony. Irony is a whole dialect here, within which you can still be funny, moving, open, generous, sincere. Second, since I have little in the way of an inner life, my resting state is a deep boredom, and New York is the least boring place I know.

New York's great secret – or rather, the truth it cannot openly declare – is that it is the European capital of your dreams. Lord knows, it isn't really America. I'm always bewildered by friends who visit, and then plan five things to do every day – a gallery, a trip to Katz's Deli, a show … They're missing the point. The city is the show. Architecturally, for example, its brutal grid serves only to highlight its insane, principled, obsessive variety. No two adjacent buildings are the same; and no building embodies the beauty and lunacy of the place like the Frick Collection, a jaw-dropping limestone pile taking up a whole block at the corner of

70th Street and Fifth Avenue. It's never long before I wind up here, as often by blind instinct as by design. (For others, it's not the art that makes it a place of pilgrimage. Every casual geek will tell you that Batman's Gotham City is "Manhattan below 14th Street at 11 minutes past midnight on the coldest night in November", but less well known is the fact that the Avengers' mansion is the Frick: 890 Fifth Avenue is the same address as 1 East 70th.)

Henry Clay Frick (1849–1919) was a pretty dreadful piece of work. He made his money in the coke industry – not the one that underwrites the hedge funders who now make up half the Upper West Side, but the black stuff – and his first million before he turned 30. He invested in the railways, became a business partner of Andrew Carnegie and was soon supremely wealthy. But even the film they play in the Frick's Music Room can't entirely avoid mentioning one of a number of shameful events that gave him his reputation for unscrupulous ruthlessness. The movie judiciously skirts round his response to the Johnstown Flood, when an ill-conceived fishing lake designed for Frick, Carnegie and his other cronies burst its banks and flooded the valley below, killing thousands. Although he made some token compensation, Frick ensured that all efforts to hold the South Fork Fishing and Hunting Club responsible were foiled (the victims' failure to secure damages led directly to changes in American law on liability). But the film does touch on his breaking of the Homestead Steel Strike of 1892, which ended with the death of several steelworkers – and an assassination attempt on Frick shortly after.

When Frick finally left Pittsburgh for New York, it was initially to reside in the Vanderbilt mansion on Fifth. The Vanderbilts were not known for their delicate touch with interior decoration, Edith Wharton going so far as to declare them "entrenched in a sort of Thermopylae of bad taste"; but whatever faults Frick had, bad taste was not one of them. He had begun as a collector of modern art, then turned his attention to the Old Masters, and had already amassed a world-class collection by the time he arrived in New York. Presumably further inspired or repulsed by the baroque excess of his temporary digs, he conceived a mansion of starkly contrasting neoclassical simplicity, to show his art to best advantage. Thomas Hastings, architect of the New York Public Library, was commissioned to design and build it, and the astonishing result was a little Petra seemingly carved from whatever giant lump of unhewn rock had once joined 70th and 71st. (It is said that Frick hoped "to make Carnegie's place look like a miner's shack". He did.)

Frick lived there only a few years before his death, and it was always his intention that the collection would be open to the public. I'd like to think that this was his guilty reparation for a life of unbridled greed, but who knows what he was thinking.

Wandering in off the street – the sirens, the shouting, the car horns used instead of brakes – you discover the architectural equivalent of a pair of Bose noise-cancelling headphones. The place is so quiet, the effect is less of silence than of deafness. How could such a still space be carved from such a noisy city? There are several answers. Most crucially, there are no kids. I love kids – mine especially – but they can ruin things. No child under ten is allowed into the Frick. This would be a horrid rule applied more generally; but shouldn't there be the occasional designated adult space, beyond bars, bookies and strip clubs?

The second thing keeping the peace is the visitors' own Trappist silence: this museum attracts a class of folk who do not want their own concentration disturbed, and so will not disturb yours. And the third is plain, old-fashioned awe. The Frick astonishes because there are few surprises; it barely contains a single painting that will not already be familiar to you. The only surprise is that they are all here. Well spaced, breathing freely, often arranged by no other organising principle than supremely good taste, in uncluttered rooms of perfect classical dimensions.

I first came here about 23 years ago. I was living in Brighton with a girl from Brooklyn, and we were still in love enough to want to impress each other, competitively. I showed her the Scottish Highlands; she showed me the Brooklyn Bridge. I took her to Edinburgh's Princes Street Gardens; she took me to the Frick, and won. These days, I'm really here for my half-dozen favourite paintings, and deliberately take the most circuitous route I can towards them. This often involves an aimless half-hour in the beautiful Garden Court, all marble and foliage and fountains; it was once an open courtyard, but was covered and enclosed after Frick's death. The work was accomplished so seamlessly it's impossible to believe it didn't form part of the original house. I defy anyone to see it, and not have it form part of their vision of an afterlife.

The day I visit, there's also a Renoir exhibition, so I go to see that first. Why does anyone like Renoir? Every canvas looks like a ten-foot biscuit tin. I take a sort of refuge in Corot's *The Lake*. It's both a terrific painting and an absolute downer, which I return to again and again for reasons I cannot explain. A yellowy-brown monochrome watercolour-in-oils, its light is bleary, blurry, heavy, sodden, purgatorial. The cattle look bewildered and lost. It reminds me intensely of my depressions, which I am largely free of these days. Perhaps I love it because I know I can turn my back on it. I head for the Fragonard Room, confident that if this can't cheer me up, nothing will.

The Fragonard Room is the clearest piece of evidence that this is a house built with art in mind. Plans for a drawing room were altered to accommodate a series of wonderful, ridiculous panels depicting the Progress of Love. Against the backdrop of an impossibly rococo arcadia, an assortment of beribboned, bewigged, pomaded and pantalooned twerps and nincompoops spoon and sport. Below a statue of Cupid, a woman swoons in a dégagé reverie, her eyes rolled up to the whites. Banksy would have added a hypodermic needle dangling from her arm. You feel deeply protective of these figures. They depict a heaven, of sorts, though not one to which we should aspire.

And then, like an old friend, I see Constable's *Salisbury Cathedral from the Bishop's Grounds*. This painting is missing the ugly rack of cloud that looms in the V&A version, and I agree with Bishop John Fisher that this approach is a big improvement. The trees have the weird underlight of coming storm, which renders the pale cathedral and its infinite spire perfectly radiant, and straightforwardly mystical. From the other side of the room, I always think I'm approaching a Samuel Palmer. The painting seems to generate more and more natural detail before your eyes, in an almost fractal way, as a result of your own deeper looking: this is still the old, wild, pullulating English countryside, capable of the spontaneous creation of life. The effect is enhanced by Constable's having painted this more quickly than his first version, so the natural impressionism you see in his watercolours is evident in the more hastily sketched detail. One cow has been painted as glass, with the grass still visible through it. It looks more cow-like than ever.

The Frick also has my least and my second favourite Vermeer. (The one I love most is *The Lacemaker*, which I caught at the Fitzwilliam recently, in a room so busy I saw one guy looking at it through binoculars.) My least favourite is Burn Handing a Folded Map of the London Underground to Man in Drag, otherwise known as *Mistress and Maid*. This was the last painting Frick bought, and one of his favourites. Maybe I'm just trying to disagree about something. But the expressions of both women are, to me at least, so open to interpretation as to be not worth troubling over. I ask myself all the questions I have been instructed to ask. Is the note from a lover? How much does the servant know? What does the lady's chin-hand gesture mean? Who knows? Who cares?

Officer and Laughing Girl, on the other hand, is the one I'd leave with under my jacket. How can this be not now? Never has someone looked so convincingly entertained, captivated, alive. Just like the cock-and-bull story he's telling, the officer looms too large in the foreground. There's a theory that this may have been a distortion introduced by Vermeer's use of the camera obscura, but heavens, does it work. Everything lives in that picture. Even the light gathering in the carved scoops of the window frame shouts, "Today!" The upside-down and thoroughly unreliable map of Holland on the wall serves to remind us that everything changes, and nothing changes at all.

Isn't it odd how you feel the presence of some artists almost before you see them? Frick was a sucker for a strong personality. You know the Ingres by the stare of the Comtesse d'Haussonville on the back of your neck, the Piero della Francesca by the ghostly clump of John the Evangelist's big, solid feet, the Turners from their focal blaze in the corner of your eye. But one painting seems to work by sheer physical magnetism, and reminds me of the real reason I keep coming back here: Bellini's *St Francis in the Desert*. And then I remember the reason I keep coming back to the Bellini.

Michael Donaghy was a poor Irish boy from the Bronx, the product of the kind of household that would have done its kids a lot less damage if it had divorced. But, as his namesake Jack

Donaghy (played by Alec Baldwin) once said in *30 Rock*, "The Irish
mate for life. Like swans. Like drunk, angry swans." His loving,
violent upbringing left Michael a neurotic, ethereal, infinitely
sweet man, much too sensitive to suffer this bruising planet for
the full term. He was a polymath, who read everything and was
incapable of forgetting any of it. He would go through periods so
book-obsessed he would not watch his dreams but read them.
He claimed to have run with a gang called the Bronx Philologists,
and bought his drugs from a guy called Schwa. He made a lot of
stuff up. He was also one of the finest poets of the age. I loved him
dearly, and suffered his death as I would a brother's.

His head, as they say in Dundee, was full of doors, all banging.
The doorless silences of the Frick created a place of asylum for
Michael. A keen student of the Italian Renaissance, his poetry is
full of references and buried allusions to the masters. *St Francis in
the Desert* was his favourite painting, and he would stand entranced
before it, hour after hour. The trance was often heavily drug-
induced. On one occasion, he told me, he spent the afternoon
helplessly frozen in Francis's own pose – until he was physically
removed from the premises, the complaint that he was about to
receive the stigmata falling on deaf ears.

The Bellini really is a grand thing to stand in front of for an
hour, and the miracle is that you can still actually do this, in New
York, at lunchtime, largely without human interruption. Everything in the picture is, you soon notice, turned towards the glory
off-stage. The crane, the distant turrets, the skull on Francis's
desk, even the slow, dumb donkey: all are helplessly drawn to the
unseen source. (I had this as my desktop in the late 1990s – a click-
able version on which the saint's foot opened Word, and so on.
My instinct is still to jab at his sandals to check my e-mail.)

Francis's chest-forward, open-armed pose has more than a

touch of Eric Cantona about it – someone basking proudly in the glory as much as humbly before it, accepting as much as he is rendering. It makes me think of what Rilke meant when he described us as "receivers": less passive recipients of the Word than active listeners for it, less pocket radio than Very Large Array. After half an hour I move out of Donaghy's shade and leave him standing there, tuned in, at last, to a pure and noiseless signal, and blissfully invisible to the security guards. And I head back out into the chaos and car horns of Fifth Avenue, relieved that I still know where to find him.

The Frick Collection
1 East 70th Street, New York, NY 10021, United States
www.frick.org

The Wings of Capri

VILLA SAN MICHELE, CAPRI

Ali Smith

Early in 2011 I stood in the sculpture loggia at the Villa San Michele in Anacapri, and I didn't just look a god in the eye, I poked a god in the eye. Even better: I cleaned out the eye of a god. I leaned forward under the green bronze head of a Mercury looking down at me, one wing spread open on the side of his head, and removed a small piece of cobweb from the hollow of one of his eyes.

Then I stepped back and wrote in my notebook, "maybe one of the few museums in the world still able to let you be human around its exhibits." I wrote, and then I realised the table I was leaning on was an exhibit too, a table I'd actually read about, knew a story about. Its surface, a slab of beautiful inlaid fragments of multicoloured marble, was the opposite side of a piece of rough stone used as a washboard for decades, maybe centuries, by Sicilian washerwomen. One day at the end of the 19th century Axel Munthe, the man who built and put this house together, saw the women doing their washing. The next time he passed them he brought a brand-new turn-of-the-20th-century washboard, jumped out of his carriage and offered it in exchange for the slab. The women were delighted.

Now, more than 100 years later, I was leaning on it, and nobody was running to tell me not to. Was the story about this table true? So many of Munthe's stories about the history of the contents of his villa are, shall we say, a bit dubious. This head of Mercury, for instance, eyeing me now. A spider-eaten piece of worthless junk? Or something really truly old?

It didn't matter – or rather, it wasn't what mattered. I was high up on Capri, whose rearing rock bluffs rise out of the sea into a choreography of cloud and cliff, a never-ending shape-shift between mist and revelation. Now you see, and now you don't. Capri has a way of letting you see differently. A "dreaming sphinx", Munthe noted in his travel journal in 1885; that's what the poets called Capri, an "antique sarcophagus". A sarcophagus? All this light, all this greenness and air and life? The most beautiful place I've ever been, in a vast fall of sky and sea of a blue not even Giotto could equal: an old tomb?

Munthe was a doctor, a man who'd lost count of the mounting corpses of the poor in the Naples cholera epidemic. He first came to this bright island as a very young man, aged 19, in 1876, under the shadow of consumption. So Death isn't just a concept, it's a character with a capital D in Munthe's *The Story of San Michele* (1929). This charming, irascible, rich, mad and funny memoir went on to be translated into about 40 languages and to sell 25 million copies. It made Munthe and his villa world-famous, though it's really more shaggy-dog than true, and more about his young life as a doctor and psychiatrist in Paris and Rome than it is about this place, the old house and ruined chapel on the site of a Tiberian villa, which he bought from the local carpenter in 1895 and transformed into the Villa San Michele. It sits on a cliff edge, over which, according to legend, the Roman emperor Tiberius liked to tip the boys, girls, men and women he'd finished with and watch them fall. The view over the Bay of Naples, Sorrento and Vesuvius is a thing of near-shocking beauty.

Munthe wanted to make a home "open to sun and wind and

the voice of the sea, like a Greek temple, and light, light, light everywhere". But he was a man with a lifelong eye problem; the brightness of Anacapri would be a kind of torture to him for the 40 years he lived here. So he had darker glasses made, bought a shady old tower for when San Michele would be too much and set to work.

> The whole garden was full of thousands and thousands of polished slabs ... all now forming the pavement of the big loggia, the chapel and some of the terraces. A broken cup of agate of exquisite shape, several broken and unbroken Greek vases, innumerable fragments of Roman sculpture ... came to light ... While we were planting the cypresses bordering the little lane to the chapel, we came upon a tomb with the skeleton of a man, he had a Greek coin in his mouth, the bones are still there where we found them, the skull is lying on my writing table.

His book is a cheeky, headlong mess of arrogance and modesty, a northern magic-realism transposed on the hot south, all dreams, tall stories, garrulous ghosts. Written between the world wars, picking its way across "the dangerous No Man's Land between fact and fancy", it opens with flowers and beautiful girls and ends with a paean to the songs and the wings of birds. From beginning to end it's a revelation both of Munthe's spirit and of his tendency to make truth up as he went along. He built the villa by eye, he swears, without an architect (this isn't true: the architect's plans are in the house's archives). He found the great granite statue of the sphinx, which gazes out to sea at the garden's outermost point, by following a panpipe-playing shepherd in a dream (there's a receipt for the sphinx in the house's archives; it came from a Naples antiques dealer). As he says, near the start: "I do not ask for better than not to be believed."

Unbelievable, larger than life, and a maker of life itself into something larger, he was the kind of man who'd buy a mountain just to stop the practice of bird-snaring on it. (Capri is a resting spot for the world's migratory birds; thanks to the animal-loving, bird-revering Munthe the hill above Villa San Michele, for centuries a hub of quail hunt and blood sport, is now an important bird sanctuary.) An expert in the manipulation of the lethargic rich, he was also a volunteer in the outbreaks of cholera and typhus among the poor. A foreigner taken to heart by the locals, he was more intimate than a doctor should really be with his most illustrious patient, Victoria, the crown princess, later queen, of Sweden. He made his name via the rich and famous, refused money from the impoverished, and was happy to be paid, as he once was, in the shape of a full-grown, alcohol-dependent baboon.

Over the years the villa, with its eccentric mix of "dug-up" or "found" Roman and Greek artefacts and its hotchpotch of royalty, locals, dogs, cats, hens, dipsomaniac monkeys and resident mongoose, became a place of fashionable pilgrimage. Henry James called it "a creation of the most fantastic beauty, poetry and inutility I have ever seen clustered together". Oscar Wilde came, not long out of prison (Munthe was among the few across Europe to be kind to him). Rilke visited. The famously unsociable Garbo actually volunteered herself for a visit ("surprisingly nice", Munthe noted). History itself visited in all its contemporary guises, with Stefan Zweig consulting Munthe on the best ways to commit suicide and Hermann Goering consulting him about buying the Villa (Munthe politely refused). On his death in 1949 he left the building, its gardens and the mountain behind to the Swedish state, and now as well as this glorious museum, bird sanctuary and a huge open-air concert space for Anacapri, it houses a near-paradisal colony of studios with fellowships for Swedish artists.

I first came here in November 1995; I had just won some money in a short-story competition, and because I was thinking of maybe writing something about Pompeii (it would turn out to be my first novel), my partner and I came to visit the remains and look in the mouth of the volcano. One day on a whim we caught the ferry from Sorrento to Capri, where Gracie Fields and Graham Greene had both lived, which was pretty much all I knew about it. We arrived in the Marina Grande, small and excitingly ramshackle. There was a funicular railway running up the side of the mountain, so we got on. Then we boarded a bus which took us up a ribbon of road too small for a bus and let us off in a tiny white village square. We followed our noses down a shop-lined road, and came to a Moorish-looking building. In we went – by chance exactly 100 years after Munthe bought the land from Master Vincenzo, the carpenter.

I remember being intrigued by it, loving it. Now, 16 years later, I'm coming back for the first time. It's warm, somewhere between spring and summer, and I'm older, if not much wiser, in that I think I know where I'm going and what I'm likely to see there: a sphinx or two, a beautiful garden, a house full of fragments, a really amazing view. It's a place that the writer Bruce Chatwin compared to Pasadena and Beverly Hills for its cheap gaudiness; a rich man's play-place from the turn of the last century, Chatwin thought.

But something a bit beyond me is already happening. The ferry journey from Naples to Capri has left my chest feeling more open. I hadn't actually noticed it was closed.

Now everywhere, all through the pristine old house, I can't help seeing things with wings, Mercury after Mercury, and not just Mercuries, there are winged fragmented feet, winged beings, winged heads, the stone-carved wings of birds in the old fragments fixed into the walls. Then as I walk through the house and out towards the statues and garden what happens, in a word, is birdsong.

It's as if the air is electrically alive with it. It's like hearing your own ear waken. I move back into the study for a moment. A lot of people walk past me – one of the curious things about the Villa San Michele is that although it's pretty busy, nothing feels crowded – and I listen, first to the birdsong at the back of everything, then to what the people say, in all the languages, every time the house springs its surprise of openness and light on them. Oh. Look.

That's what it's like to visit the Axel Munthe Museum. You walk through a hall, a kitchen, a bedroom, a study, a place to live that's lined and scattered with fragments of art, junk, beauty, history. Then you find yourself on a path that gets lighter and lighter; then art, junk, history, home, trees, stone, leaves and sky all shift together on the edge of a view so open that it renews the very word "view" itself. I'm laughing at my own inadequacy, at the inadequacy of memory, but most of all at how cunning this place is, making you open your eyes, ears, senses, leading you through from space to open space until finally you hit it, it hits you – a kind of blue infinity, an epitome of openness.

I walk up the path. Two French kids dodge past me. Birdsong and laughter. I go and visit the old red and black granite sphinx overlooking the bay, the one Munthe found "in a dream". I run my hand over her shiny flank. You can't see her face unless you're a bird. I double back and visit the other, the little Etruscan winged sphinx silhouetted against the sheer drop; the lichen growing on this sphinx is a very bright yellow and the ships below her and all the houses on the mountain are nothing but tiny white flecks, the size of flakes of sea salt. I come back through the sculpture loggia; the bowed heads of the busts are ceremonious, resigned. I revisit Munthe's study, with the huge stone head of Medusa above his writing desk. His dictionary, Swedish–English, is open at the words for "closeness", "charlatan", "remains".

A sprightly elderly lady sits down near me for a moment, to get her breath. She tells me she is from Holland and that she read *The Story of San Michele* 50 years ago and loved it, then read it again six years ago and decided, finally, to come. Why did she wait 50 years? She shrugs. "Life comes," she says. Four children, a husband, 40 years as a doctor herself, then the body gets old. She hits at one of her swollen-looking feet with her walking stick. She tells me her name is Marijke, and that the writing room is her favourite place. She likes what he says about how we should eat, drink, be merry, "but he was dark too, a misanthrope". You think? I say. "I think, you know, he was in a relationship with death," she says. We both look over at the huge grave Medusa head on the wall.

Munthe claimed he had found the Medusa at the bottom of the sea. Somewhere over time it's lost its snakes, its eyebrows, even one of its eyelids. Today it's garlanded with fresh ivy, very green, very alive.

Maybe he wanted to be turned to stone, I say. Marijke makes a small gesture that takes in all the stonework around us. She shrugs, gets to her feet, smiles, shakes my hand and goes out into the light.

It reminds me of something Shirley Hazzard says in her sparkling memoir about this island and about her friend Graham Greene, *Greene on Capri*. She quotes from an Italian novel, something she thinks is true not just about being here, in this almost unbearably beautiful place, but about Greene, his art, and the business of being human. "Human beings need unhappiness at least as much as they need happiness." The mercurial Munthe, the old charlatan, knew the shifts and contraries of it, I think, standing here in this little piece of Sweden in Italy, this piece of the north in the south, with its garden full of tourists where you can still, regardless, feel solitary and unhurried, its museum without labels, freed up from all the categories. He brings the sky into the house, turns you towards a horizon, suggests that "real" and "fake" is missing the point. He understood – above all from his own troubled eyesight – that in a place of such brightness, colour and light, the riddle more than ever involves the dark. He didn't want museumry, he wanted the puckish act, the live shape-shift, the act of the imagination. That's what this place built on its cliff-edge is about. So I was standing next to Mercury, god of thieves, artists, storytellers, communication, the underworld path between the dead and the living. There was a cobweb; it looked like quite a fresh one. Would anyone mind, I wondered, if I reached up and removed it?

I poked my finger into the hollow eye of the god. Then I went out to take one more look at infinity.

Villa San Michele
Viale Axel Munthe 34, 80071 Anacapri, Italy
www.villasanmichele.eu

Spurned No Longer

NATIONAL GALLERY OF VICTORIA, MELBOURNE

Tim Winton

As you approach the National Gallery of Victoria, along a boulevard jangling with trams in downtown Melbourne, it's easy to see why a former director called it "the Kremlin of St Kilda Road". It's a massive rectangular block whose bluestone walls have something of the penitentiary about them, and in a quarter teeming with tourists and commuters it manages to retain a perpetual and sinister remoteness. There are no windows. The only break in the mass is a portal arch so tiny that it could be a mousehole in *Tom and Jerry*. Only when you step into that entryway do you see the building's inner skin. There's no portcullis here. All that stands between you and Australia's greatest art collection is a falling sheet of water. The water wall has been disarming pedestrians and delighting children since the museum's unveiling in 1968. Today, on a hot morning in the summer holidays, kids linger to feel the current sluice through their fingers. It's a treat to watch them. It takes me back.

You could say the NGV and I got off to an awkward start. Back then, nearly half a century ago, the new building on St Kilda Road had been open less than a year; it was Melbourne's new civic triumph, a trophy the city's burghers and bohemians could share and dispute over. But I was of neither tribe. I arrived at her door sweaty and barefoot, a scruffy nine-year-old interloper from the western frontier.

I was born and raised in far-flung Western Australia, where the desert meets the sea. With the Indian Ocean at its feet and some of the world's most inhospitable terrain looming in the rear, Perth is a city under geographical siege. It was long referred to as the most isolated city in the world and locals seized upon this distinction with a mix of shame, resentment and defensive pride. I grew up in a hardy, utilitarian environment, where nobody you knew had ever finished school; where practical skills were valued; and beauty, art and language were mere frippery. It seemed there was a cultural moat between me and the speculative dream-world I learned to call art. But there were larger barriers to contend with – distance chief among them. The "real" Australia, the one we saw on TV and in magazines, lay elsewhere, somewhere beyond the heat haze of the treeless plain. It was hard not to feel that everything you knew was inconsequential.

Feeling overlooked, even spurned by the eastern states (which made up two-thirds of the land mass), westerners like me suffered the prickly anxiety felt by provincials the world over. We dreamt of making the great crossing to the Other Side, if only to confirm it wasn't all it was cracked up to be. The trip across the Nullarbor was a rite of passage, and in those days it was quite an undertaking – not simply because of the distances involved (Perth is much farther from Melbourne than London from Moscow), but because the only road linking the west to the rest was a brutal limestone track that ate cars and sent motorists nutty. My family made the trek in the summer of 1969, juddering across the corrugations by day, coughing white dust, camping under the stars by the roadside when we could take no more. The desert heat was intense and the landscape austere and pitiless.

We were sure our ordeals would not be in vain. Keen for us to experience the great world beyond, my parents had taken us out of school early. There was, they said, so much to see and do and learn, and Melbourne was a town where things happened. We'd visit the hallowed stands of the Melbourne Cricket Ground, walk the streets where cop shows like *Homicide* and *Division 4* were recorded in glorious black-and-white, and finally, most importantly, we'd tarry in the shadow of the Sidney Myer Music Bowl, where only a year or two earlier the legendary Seekers had played a homecoming concert to 200,000 fans, the largest audience in Australia's history.

It took more than a week to reach Melbourne. We knocked the dust from our clothes and worked our way through the sites of pilgrimage and, though no one would admit it, our hearts were sinking. The place looked ordinary. The trams were jaunty in their anachronistic way, but nothing about Melbourne looked any more potent or Australian than the places we knew. The MCG was just a hulk. The scene of the Seekers' triumph, without our white-bread troubadours to enliven it, didn't have much to excite a nine-year-old. Even Mum and Dad seemed a tad underwhelmed, but they lingered dutifully at the foot of the stage as we kids chased up the freshly mown amphitheatre towards the final stop on the itinerary.

Mum had shown me pictures of the brand-new museum: by all accounts the place was terribly modern. But that hot day, footsore as we were, its chief promise was water. We bolted through the parkland from the Myer Bowl to the fortress on St Kilda Road, and there, for a moment, we stood awed before the gallery's moat-like ponds. Then, like the heathens we were, we dunked our feet and were happier than we'd been all day. To me the water was special relief. I'd stubbed both big toes and the flapping scabs were a nuisance. Even before our parents arrived, adults were

sooling us out of the water. Dunking, they said, was disrespect-
ful. Didn't we know this was art?

Once we'd dried off on the hot pavement, we knew better
than to touch the tantalising sheets of the water wall that lay like a
shimmering curtain between the street and the mysteries within.
We fell into line and followed our parents through the great portal
arch into the cool interior. We were on our best behaviour. Mum
spat on her thumb and cleaned our faces.

And then we presented ourselves at the box office, only to
learn that we would not be admitted. Barefoot supplicants were
not welcome in the temple of art. Mum was shamed; we were
mortified. But there was worse to come because Dad was irritated
and determined to press the point. Fine for him, safely shod in his
rubber thongs, but for the rest of us, shrunk back in ignominy, it
was awful. After trying several dud approaches, he made a break-
through. He told the attendant we were from Queensland – and
suddenly all resistance ceased. It seemed that for yokels from the
tropic north they'd make allowances. We were in!

It was a victory nearly wasted: I was so embarrassed I could
barely absorb what lay before me. And this is how I came to be
acquainted with Henry Moore. For many minutes I lurked behind
his *Draped Seated Woman*, trying to regain some composure. It
could have been a parked car for all I cared. Still, I had time to take
it in, and there was something consoling in its mass. Its curves
were confusingly voluptuous. It was, as Mum had promised, terribly modern, but there was a quality to it I later recognised as
humane. I didn't just take shelter from it; I took heart. And from
there I set off to see what else I could find.

I roamed free. In the great hall I craned to take in Leonard
French's much-discussed stained-glass ceiling. It would have been
great to lie on the floor to see it better, but I didn't dare. From there

I wandered the courts and galleries, seeking out local legends like Tom Roberts and Frederick McCubbin, whose colonial images were familiar from school. I lingered at Russell Drysdale's *The Rabbiters*: it sounded traditional, and its colours looked old-timey, but it seemed weird, almost haunted. Was this modern? I didn't know. I couldn't stop looking at it. In the halls of the European masters I was all at sea. I stopped only to take in works that were monumental or whose artists were famous enough to ring a bell. Like Rembrandt, whose *Two Old Men Disputing* brought to mind a pair of cricket fanatics in a care home. It was a picture you fell into. You could look at it for the rest of your life and still wonder what the story was.

There were many things I didn't understand, stuff that made me uneasy, stripes and splashes and globs on pedestals that had me scratching my head. There seemed to be no limit to what people could think of. And that was a giddy feeling. On and on the galleries went, on and on I trekked, until finally I yielded in dismay, back-tracked like a sunburnt Hansel and found my clan hunkered by the entrance, spent and waiting.

Passing back through the water wall to the familiar world, I had a dim sense I'd seen something special. I knew I was no genius but I didn't want to be ordinary and if I'd learned anything from the excursion it was what people could do when they saw past the everyday. There was no single experience that made me want to live by my imagination, but I don't doubt the pivotal effect this visit had. Within a year I was telling anyone who'd listen that I was going to be a writer.

So it was a treat, in the summer of 2015, to return to the NGV, no longer a new sensation, now an institution. There have been changes. The palazzo-style building on St Kilda Road has been rebadged as the NGV International, and the handsome Australian collection has been rehoused at the Ian Potter Centre across the Yarra. Recent renovations have afforded the old building more exhibition space, and I found the halls teeming with visitors. From the exterior it's still quite daunting, but the museum-going public is not as easily intimidated as it once was. That sullen reverence has fallen away. Children and their parents run their hands delightedly up the cascading sheets of the water wall. It's a pleasure to see ordinary folks reaching out, making contact, claiming the place as they enter.

Inside the democratic spirit continues. Nowadays admission to the permanent collection is free. Children are welcomed without reservation. The morning of my visit, kids were lined up to ride the glittering brass carousel in the central court. In the Great Hall, where Leonard French's 51-metre stained-glass ceiling remains, they lay on the floor, pointing and writhing. It was a joy to see a grandmother shuck her shoes and chase her charges from one end of the hall to the other in her bare feet.

Sadly, the ceiling itself hasn't fared well with the years. Caught at the wrong moment, it looks like the world's largest crocheted rug ready to be spread across the knees of a giant philanthropist. Henry Moore's once controversial *Draped Seated Woman* is still there, handy as ever, even if the face on her pin head now seems disrespectfully blank.

Close by in the new sculpture garden is Pino Conte's *Tree of Life*, featuring an infant clinging stubbornly to its mother's breast. This babe could be any age. The mother's arboreal trunk is sensually rendered but her mass is implacable. It's a lovely, muscular celebration of the life-urge and if I were to bring one of my grandkids to the NGV, this would be our first stop. In the labyrinth of the European galleries, noticing for the first time what a solid collection of religious art the museum has amassed, I came upon Titian's *Monk with a Book*. A pious man might prefer to be seen looking heavenward, but our friar has been caught seeking some action closer to home. Rembrandt's *Two Old Men Disputing* is still there, luminous as ever, and farther along, in the gallery dedicated to 17th- and 18th-century works, I met a new acquisition – Jean-François Sablet's gorgeous portrait of Daniel Kervégan, mayor of Nantes, a revolution-era burgher rendered with rare sympathy. His is the face of a plain, trustworthy man with tired, soulful eyes. Here is the sort of citizen-leader the communards dreamt of. But even in this world-weary visage there's no hint of the Terror to come.

With the familiar past behind me, I rested over a pot of Darjeeling and reflected on the changes that have come to the museum. Apart from the structural additions, about which I have mixed feelings, the most telling improvements are social. The courts of the David Shrigley show were thick with kids drawing responses to the work. Upstairs, the young and curious coursed through galleries, snapping and texting. The temple of art no longer spurns the uninitiated.

In the collection, the most telling change is the growing prominence of Asian art. When I was a kid, Australia had barely begun to emerge from the moral murk of the White Australia Policy, and the NGV's collection remained trenchantly Europhile. At the entrance to the growing Asian collections is a smouldering piece by an Indonesian artist, Haris Purnomo. *Orang Hilang*, a work of remembrance for the disappeared activists of the Suharto years, has the happy effect of inoculating the occidental viewer against narrowly ethnographic expectations. Yes, the galleries feature works of tradition and antiquity – like the Jin Dynasty Guanyin and many precious ceramics from Japan and China – but there's a growing appetite for contemporary exemplars and Purnomo's piece helps set the tone. An old man with a limpid stare and a telling scar at the base of his neck wears the names of the missing like wounds. Words are too dangerous to utter. His mouth is covered. His eyes and a patchwork of plasters speak for him.

For all its naked political intent, it's a beautiful object, and of all the paintings it's the one I saw people linger over longest. I stayed all day and tasted but a fraction of what was on offer. Following the kids and their guardians out through the water wall, I thought again of that boyhood visit. I first entered the NGV barefoot and cowering, but I was so taken with what I saw that I forgot to be embarrassed. I strode out of the place like a man in boots.

National Gallery of Victoria
180 St Kilda Road, Melbourne VIC 3006, Australia
www.ngv.vic.gov.au

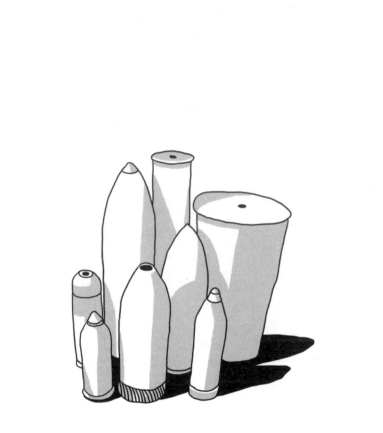

The Pity of War

Michael Morpurgo

The first time I went to Ypres, to In Flanders Fields Museum, housed in the Cloth Hall that forms one side of the town square, I was with Michael Foreman, the great illustrator. We were there to attend a conference on books for the young set against the background of war – I had written *War Horse* some years before, and Michael had written *War Boy* and *War Game*. We were already good friends, having collaborated closely on several stories. We had laughed together a great deal over the years, as friends do. Emerging into the harsh light of day after visiting In Flanders Fields Museum, we wept together.

As a schoolboy, I had read the War Poets – Wilfred Owen and Siegfried Sassoon, Edward Thomas and Edmund Blunden (who was a friend of my stepfather's and often stayed with us at weekends). I had heard Britten's *War Requiem*, and read *All Quiet on the Western Front*, and seen the film. I'd worn my poppy every autumn, stood cocooned in silence for two minutes every Remembrance Day. But none of these things touched me so intensely as this museum.

Since that first visit, I've been back several times: sometimes to research other stories set in the first world war, such as *Private Peaceful*; sometimes to perform these stories in folk-song concerts in village halls and churches all over Flanders. I feel I belong here. My grandfather Emile Cammaerts was Belgian: too old to fight in

1914, he boosted the morale of his compatriots by writing poems, some later set to music by Elgar. Ypres has become a place of pilgrimage for me. And always, when I step out into the bustle of the town square after passing once more through In Flanders Fields, I find myself lost in sadness.

On one visit I saw some English teenagers piling out of a coach to visit a cemetery just outside Ypres. As they wandered off into the field of ghosts, their loudness and laughter died, their hearts suddenly and deeply troubled by the endless rows of "Portland stone bonnet" gravestones with their bleak inscriptions: "Sergeant James Macdonald. Scots Guards. September 7th 1915. Gone." These youngsters had probably read Owen's words about "the pity of war". Now they could comprehend something of what he meant, something of what he felt. It is the pity that wrenches the heart.

Just before Christmas, I came back to this same place, the Bedford House Cemetery, and to In Flanders Fields Museum. This time, Maggie Fergusson, literary editor of *Intelligent Life* and a friend with whom I am working on a book about my life, came too, bringing Flora, her 12-year-old daughter. Flora was seeing all this for the first time, so I tried to talk her through it, to explain how the war began, how it was waged; to rationalise what we were seeing all around us.

In the cemetery, perhaps, it was some use for her to have me there. I did what I could to set the graves in some kind of historical context. It helped that we had also visited the place where the front line had once been, and had looked out over the shallow valley where the Christmas truce had taken place in 1914. It's now a wide green meadow, a farmstead with a wood beyond. A farmer's daughter was out riding her horse, a buzzard mewing above us. Nowhere could have looked more idyllically peaceful. It helped too that we had stood under the Menin Gate gazing up at the names of the soldiers who have no known grave, all 54,896 of them, and had heard the buglers of the Ypres Fire Brigade sound the Last Post, as they do every evening at eight o'clock.

But, once we were inside the museum, my role as historical guide was redundant. From the moment we entered, words and photographs, film and sound, sculpture, paintings, artefacts and models told of how, nearly a century ago, men went mad all over Europe.

There is a sense of personal involvement in all this. On entering the museum, visitors are encouraged to choose a real character whose story they can follow through the war. Walking beside me, Flora is absorbed in the life of a Dutch girl, six years old when the war broke out, and orphaned shortly afterwards.

The first floor of the Cloth Hall is made up of a series of long, dark chambers, through which the visitor is led chronologically from the build-up of hostilities in the early years of the 20th century, and the mounting horrors of the war, to eventual peace. The first words we read, engraved on a piece of stone, are by H. G. Wells: "Every intelligent person in the world knew that disaster was impending, and knew no way to avoid it." This was a colossal version of an everyday thing, the accident waiting to happen. An escalating arms race between the great powers, the ratcheting-up of belligerent rhetoric, the formation of the Triple Alliance and Triple Entente, meant that almost any spark would have been sufficient to light the fuse. The assassination of Archduke Franz Ferdinand in Sarajevo did just that. It didn't cause an immediate explosion, but in its wake armies began to manoeuvre, politicians to bluster, alarm to grow. Patriotic propaganda stirred up so much righteous indignation that ordinary people became eager for war.

The story is told simply and succinctly through newspaper headlines and archive footage. The visitor stands under a vast hanging cylinder gazing up at the faces of Europe: soldiers and civilians, victims all, about to be overwhelmed by violence. To cheering crowds, men march off to war in bright antique costumes, in helmets that would better suit Hans Christian Andersen's Brave Tin Soldier. And waiting for them, half-hidden in the corner, are the machine gun and the wire, the flamethrower and the gas masks. Ahead of us, we can hear now, deep in the gloom of the dark tunnel, the crash of exploding shells, and the distant sound of bagpipes wailing. We know what's to come. We don't want to go there. But, like the soldiers in 1914, we are mesmerised, drawn inexorably on. There is no escape.

Now we are marching through ruined Ypres (the town was reduced to rubble by shelling; the present Cloth Hall meticulously reconstructs the medieval original), and on into the trenches, where the mud and the wire of No Man's Land soon stretch for 400 miles, from Switzerland to the English Channel. We are plunged almost into darkness, engulfed by the sound of shellfire. A group sculpture of soldiers, one French, one German, one Belgian, one British, sits ironically around a tea set used at the front by the British commander, General Haig. A case displays the sabre that belonged to Prince Maurice of Battenberg, cousin of King George V, killed in October 1914 fighting on the British side, and buried in Ypres town cemetery. From the walls, photographs of soldiers stare down, by no means all alike. Men from more than 30 countries fought in this war, endured life in the trenches, the cold, the lice, the rats, the shelling, the sniper fire. A whistle blows. On old footage, we watch them scramble over the top. The death rattle of machine guns punctuates the horror.

So when, round a corner, we come face to face with German

and British soldiers shaking hands in No Man's Land on Christmas Eve, 1914, it is intensely moving. Contemporary accounts displayed on the walls tell how the truce began: the tentative approach as men ventured out of their trenches to share sausages and schnapps, to talk, to smoke, to swap buttons and badges, and eventually to play a game of football. Final score: Fritz 3, Tommy 2. No change there, then.

"One Englishman was playing on the harmonica of a German lad," Joseph Werzel writes to his parents in Germany, "some were dancing ... Hated and embittered enemies were singing carols around the tree. Christmas 1914 will remain unforgettable for me."

Briefly, the sound of shelling is replaced with the murmur of the carols "Stille Nacht" and "While Shepherds Watched", exchanged between the trenches. At my side, Flora is filled with angry incomprehension: "How could the soldiers have gone back to killing each other after that? Why didn't they just say, 'Sorry, we've made friends now. We won't fight any more'?"

I draw her attention to a strange, prophetic letter written by Winston Churchill to his wife a month before the truce, in November 1914: "What would happen, I wonder, if the armies of both sides suddenly and simultaneously went on strike and said some other method must be found for settling the dispute?" The Christmas truce was the nearest they came to it: a last glimmer of hope before the bloodletting resumed.

Frequently in this museum the words of the soldiers themselves tell the story, and all too often their words are deeply troubling. Julian Grenfell writes home in a letter from the trenches, "Then the German behind put his head up again. He was laughing and talking. I saw his teeth glistening against my foresight, and I pulled the trigger very steady. He just gave a grunt and crumpled up." Grenfell's insouciance is chilling. "I adore war," he confesses. "It is like a picnic without the objectlessness of a picnic."

When you have read this, the shock of the audio-visual experience that follows is profound. The pipes are still calling, and we find ourselves standing surrounded by heads in gas masks, hanging, staring at us. A voice recites Wilfred Owen's "Dulce et Decorum Est", written six months before his death in 1918, and ending:

> My friend, you would not tell with such high zest
> To children ardent for some desperate glory,
> The old Lie: Dulce et decorum est
> Pro patria mori.

Then comes "In Flanders Fields" (1915), by John McCrae:

> We are the Dead. Short days ago
> We lived, felt dawn, saw sunset glow,
> Loved and were loved, and now we lie
> In Flanders fields.

Flora recites the poem, speaking softly, word perfect. She has learned it at primary school.

After this, there is an ache in the throat as we face, in the next room, the sculpture of a horse rearing under fire, hind legs plunged in the mud, enduring alongside the soldiers. There is an echo, for me, of *War Horse*, my story of the universal suffering of the war seen through the eyes of a horse – a story brought to astonishing life by the National Theatre. We cannot stand and stare. We are now under constant bombardment – a bombardment of statistical information, and of the personal accounts of soldiers from all sides, of doctors and nurses and refugees bombed out of their homes. Flora points out the words of a Flemish girl, her age exactly, who wrote, after visiting a local field hospital in

1917: "There were 30 or 40 soldiers who had been gassed. They lay in a room; they were burnt. One of them had an old shoe on, the others hardly anything left on, half a sleeve of a jacket. That was the saddest thing I'd ever seen."

Illustrating the eyewitness accounts are photographs and film fragments, maps and models. And laid out among these is the residue of the soldiers' grief and wretchedness, the corroded archaeology of war: helmets, buckles, bullets. Unknown quantities of this dreadful paraphernalia still lie in the earth of Flanders. Every year, some 200 tonnes of unexploded shells are unearthed, and, since the war ended, they have caused 599 civilian fatalities – the last just three years ago. And buried among the shells, the tanks, the mines, are the remains of those thousands of soldiers whose names are carved on the Menin Gate.

Towards the end of the museum, two great men speak to us of their outrage with words that resonate across a century of wars. "On behalf of those who are suffering now," writes Siegfried Sassoon in July 1917, in a letter sent to a number of his friends and later read out in the House of Commons,

> I make this protest against the deception which is being practised on them; also I believe that I may help to destroy the callous complacency with which the majority of those at home regard the continuance of agonies which they do not share, and which they have not sufficient imagination to realise.

The war artist Paul Nash, who, when he first saw the landscape around Passchendaele, had described it as "a country more conceived by Dante or Poe than by nature", calls himself "a messenger who will bring back the word from the men who are fighting to those who want the war to go on for ever".

His words stand by his iconic picture of No Man's Land, and it is this image of the hell men made on earth that stays with us as we move into a brighter room full of film clips of cheering crowds, of the soldiers who came home, many wounded and scarred, and of the graves of those who did not. I long, now, for light and air. I am desperate to be out of this Golgotha. But, before the exit, we are forced to confront one final sobering exhibit: a year-by-year tally of the number of major wars in which the Red Cross has been involved around the world since the "war to end war" ended – at the last count, 126. The figure strikes me with new force: I have just returned from visiting the children of Gaza, and seeing the effects of war first-hand. Waiting at the Hamas checkpoint to pass back into Israel, I witnessed the shooting of two children, and watched as their bloody bodies were bundled into donkey carts and hurried away.

Back in the main square, the carillon from the Cloth Hall belfry rings out over the town. Churchill said of Ypres, "A more sacred place for the British race does not exist in the whole world." If Ypres was perhaps the most concentrated killing field in British history, it was a killing field for many other peoples too. If it is sacred, then it is sacred for all of them, old friend or old foe alike. And the museum has taught me that Sassoon was closer to this truth than Churchill.

We walk across the cobbles and stand for a moment in the glorious square, bright with the lights of the Christmas Fair, echoing to the sound of children's laughter from the skating rink. Ypres has grown out of the ashes, reinvented itself. The evening bugles still sound, but the local people live for now: they have to, or the thought of the suffering the town has witnessed would make them mad. In Flanders Fields Museum, and its creator, Piet Chielens, have played a vital part in helping them to come to terms with their place in history. They know, I know, and Flora now knows, that Captain Liddell Hart was right when he said of this terrible war, "It achieved little except loss."

In Flanders Fields Museum
Grote Markt 34, 8900 Ypres, Belgium
www.inflandersfields.be

Love Bade Me Welcome

THE HARVARD MUSEUM OF NATURAL HISTORY, CAMBRIDGE, MA

Ann Patchett

The people who run the Harvard Museum of Natural History astonished me by offering to open at 8am, so that the photographer and I might have the run of the place for a couple of hours before the doors officially open to all the schoolchildren in Massachusetts. In truth, I like the schoolchildren. I like the way they scream the first time they wheel around a corner and come eye to eye with the stuffed Bengal tiger; the way they then shout for a friend, who has fallen behind the pack, transfixed by the model of a goblin shark hanging from the ceiling, so that they can see the friend scream at the tiger also. The schoolchildren serve to remind us that what we're seeing is thrilling – but still, they clog up the space in front of the giraffe.

The first time I saw that giraffe was in 1983, when he was looking a little threadbare and wearing a bandage on his neck. I was 19. I had come to Harvard summer school and fallen in love with a tall boy named Jack. Jack was interested in biology, I was interested in Jack, *ergo* I was interested in biology. I went to the Museum of Comparative Zoology, vaguely understanding that Jack did some sort of work down in the basement during the school year. The museum, which is five storeys of dark red brick and Victorian sensibility, seemed to exist in marvellous disarray. I scarcely remember what I saw in 1983 because I was wondering where Jack studied and where he ate his sandwiches. I was hoping he might see me there and be impressed by my interest in the Blaschkas' glass flowers. Not even a love-struck 19-year-old could fail to register them.

By the fall Jack and I had broken up, but a few years later our paths crossed again and we picked up a friendship that has lasted 30 years. I'm guessing it has outrun all the romances from summer school that year. What he had been working on down in the basement of the MCZ was ichthyology, the study of fishes. Later he went on to get his doctorate in evolutionary biology at Stanford, concentrating on lepidoptera, the study of butterflies. I became a novelist, and went back to Harvard when I was 30 to spend a year at the Bunting Institute at Radcliffe College. Even without love to compel me towards science, I found myself going back to the MCZ again and again.

The Harvard Museum of Natural History, which is a relatively new name, and the Museum of Comparative Zoology, founded in 1859, inhabit the same building but are not the same thing. The Museum of Natural History is the place you buy a ticket for, the place with the schoolchildren. It's the public face of the 12 departments of the MCZ (ornithology, entomology, herpetology, malacology among them), the Harvard University Herbaria (once delightfully known as the Museum of Vegetable Products) and the Mineralogical and Geological Museums. Think of the Harvard Museum of Natural History as the station, while the three other museums, functioning as working research centres, represent the track and trains stretching out across the world. This is why the Harvard Museum of Natural History is my favourite museum – perhaps my favourite place, period. You can feel the science pressing in from every direction. If you see a display of 100 birds, you can be certain they were chosen from nearly 400,000 birds in the collections, and that next time you come, many of those birds will have been rotated in order to make an entirely new exhibition. There are, all told, somewhere in the neighbourhood of 21 million specimens in Harvard's collections. What you are witnessing in this public place is the tip of the biological iceberg.

But the science is not the only thing to love. There's also the fact that the museum, despite all its updates and fresh exhibits, still maintains the feel of a place that opened its doors in 1874. "It's a museum of museums," Jack said to me once, and he was exactly right. This is what museums used to be like. It isn't just that it houses the world's only mounted Kronosaurus, or that it has one of the three greatest rubellite specimens, it's that somehow generations of curators have managed to make the place feel as if it has been left alone. Once inside, it's easy to imagine how it must have been to come to this place in 1874 and see a yak for the first time, or a perfectly rendered model of a flowering cactus. In this age of 24-hour programming on the National Geographic channel, it's easy to forget that the role of such a museum was originally to show its patrons the wonders of the world. Walking through the Great Mammal Hall, I am once again struck by the tiny legs of the lesser mouse deer, the deep, furry coat of the American bison.

"The name refers to the Great Mammals," Blue Magruder tells me, "not the Great Hall." Blue, the museum's director of marketing and communications, is taking me on a tour of the place I thought I already knew. She is so perfectly suited to her job, to the museum, it's difficult to imagine her anywhere else. She's a graduate of Radcliffe College, but her relationship to the museum goes back much further than that. Her grandmother used to take her mother there as a small child. Blue took her own son. She shows me around the fish and flowers the way another person might show me through the house she'd grown up in. There's nothing about this place she doesn't know. "When they had to replace some planks in the floor,

the wood that had originally been used was too rare. It can't be har-
vested now. But there's a company that drags the Mississippi river
and finds the logs that rolled off the barges in the 1800s." She says
this as if the bottom of the Mississippi were the logical place for
anyone to look for replacement flooring, and sure enough, they
dragged up those logs, planed them into boards, and repaired the
floors. There have been many repairs over the years, most of them
made with an eye to aligning the present with the past. "They got
rid of the hot lights – they cracked the animals," Blue says. "People
would come in and say, 'It's disgraceful. Harvard needs to get a
new rhinoceros!' But they don't understand, you can't just get a
new rhinoceros. You have to fix the one you have." Eventually the
giraffe shed his bandage. Animals were put behind glass to dis-
courage the wear and tear of petting. Still, there is an appropriate
degree of shabbiness. The West Indian monk seal looks like your
great aunt's coat dragged down from the attic. As he should. These
creatures were not born yesterday.

Everything we zip past comes with a story that makes me
want to stop for the rest of the day. Up on the ceiling hang the
bones of Steller's sea cow, extinct since the 1770s, extinct just 30
years after the species was discovered. Looking up, Blue shakes
her head. "Tasted like steak, apparently." The sailors on Bering
Island off the coast of Alaska wiped them out. Extinction looms
at every turn in this place – the dodo, the auk, passenger pigeons
and Carolina parakeets, the sweet-faced Tasmanian tiger. Half of
the animals whose placards I read are never coming back.

When I admire the pink fairy armadillo, Blue says there's a
better one up ahead. Sure enough, the next one's gorgeous: a
giant armadillo, the size of a full-grown pig. "Don't quote me on
this," she says, "but I'm pretty sure that the armadillo is the only
animal to consistently give birth to bio-identical quadruplets."

"I'm not allowed to quote you on bio-identical quadruplet armadillos?"

"That should come from a scientist," she says. "Not allowed from me."

For the record, I confirmed this quote concerning armadillo reproduction in a book about the museum, and include it as my best example of how seriously they take their facts at Harvard.

Of all the wonders in the museum, nothing really matches the collection of glass flowers. Set off in a room by themselves, the flowers are housed in old-fashioned glass display cases with wooden trim. There are many discreet signs saying that the cases should not be touched or leaned on, but no guards are present to enforce the policy. Truly, the glass flowers don't make sense at first. It's only a room full of plants in glass cases, many of them flowering, many just pulled from the ground, clumps of dirt still clinging to their roots. But what appears at first to be the perfection of nature is in fact the perfection of art, the life's work of a father and son, Leopold and Rudolf Blaschka, who lived outside Dresden.

From 1887 to 1936, first Leopold, then Leopold and Rudolf, then Rudolf alone, devoted their lives to creating over 4,000 models for Harvard, all made from glass. Like everything else in the museum, this enormous collection is rotated. "Where are the rotten apples?" a woman asks frantically. It is explained to her that the apples are no longer on display, but will return soon. Personally, I want to see the small bouquet of flowers that were a gift to Elizabeth C. Ware and her daughter, Mary Lee Ware, from Leopold Blaschka, in 1889: his thanks to the women for underwriting what would become the Ware Collection of Glass Models and Plants. The bouquet too is not currently on display. I feel a certain kinship with this woman who wants to see her apples.

Twenty years after I met Jack, I had the idea of writing a novel about a Harvard student studying ichthyology in the basement of the MCZ. What if a brilliant and privileged young man was driven to study fishes? What if his father, a politician, found this completely unacceptable? The story was not Jack's story, but he was certainly my starting point. I called him up. Did he still know anyone over at the MCZ? He put me in touch with Karsten Hartel, the collections manager of ichthyology, who invited me over.

This is where the division between the Harvard Museum of Natural History and the Museum of Comparative Zoology becomes clear, because while there is a dazzling display of dozens of fishes upstairs, downstairs there are close to a million and a half fishes in jars, in coolers, dried and stacked into drawers, stuffed, mounted, and sitting on top of cabinets. This is the part of the museum open to students and scientists but not the general public. Because I also considered making my character an ornithologist, I made the rounds of that department as well, looking at nests and eggs and flat-file drawers full of countless thousands of perfectly preserved birds. I fell in love with the birds, especially the hummingbirds rolling around in boxes like loose gems, but in the end I went with the fishes in honour of my old friend. That was the start of the novel I eventually wrote called *Run*.

A few days after going back to Harvard to research this piece, I was in New York. The Frick Collection had offered to open at 8am so that a friend of mine could come in and see an exhibition – "Vermeer, Rembrandt, and Hals: Masterpieces of Dutch Painting from the Mauritshuis". She invited me along. I stood in a room that contained a single painting, Vermeer's *Girl with a Pearl Earring*, with no one there but my friend and a security guard. I couldn't help but think of the museum that had so recently opened early for me, of the delicate branch of apple blossoms the Blaschkas had made out of glass, and the gorgeous neck of the towering giraffe. It shocked me to realise that I loved the flowers and the animals more than I loved one of the most famous paintings in the world, that I loved the planked floors and glass cases more than the most spectacular house in New York City.

All I can say is that the heart wants what it wants, and for me science has become the most spectacular art. There is no arguing with Dutch painting. The light on the cheek of that girl is transcendent. I would wish for every reader the time to go to as many museums as possible. But, if there is time for only one, I would recommend the Harvard Museum of Natural History.

The Harvard Museum of Natural History
26 Oxford Street, Cambridge, MA 02138, United States
www.hmnh.harvard.edu

A Plaster Cast in Copenhagen

THORVALDSENSMUSEUM, COPENHAGEN

Alan Hollinghurst

I'd had no more than a quarter of an hour there, five years before, but it had left me with strong and peculiar memories. The works themselves, the hundreds of sculptures in plaster and marble, had been impressive, but the building that housed them was what stayed in my mind. I'd seen nothing else like it: a massive free-standing Egyptian temple, painted a bright ochre; figures moving in frescoed procession around its outer walls, cream and ochre and plum against black backgrounds; a glazed inner cloister, in which statuary gleamed or hid in stripes of sunlight and shadow; and running round it, red, green or purple rooms in enfilade, like cells or stalls, each holding a white marble hero or goddess. The inspired colour scheme of these rooms, faded and subtilised by time, was unusually striking. It continued in the long central courtyard, frescoed with soaring palm trees, where the great Danish sculptor Bertel Thorvaldsen himself was buried, as if in a northern dream of the south.

I'd been in Copenhagen for a book fair, and my Danish publisher, knowing I was interested in buildings, had urged me at least to have a glance at this "most singular" museum before catching my plane home. At the time I had barely heard of Thorvaldsen. The museum's collection was evidence of a major artistic figure, if not exactly of a major artistic personality. The neoclassical idiom of his work, with its idealising reliance on antiquity, lacked the kind of expressive individuality that I felt I most prized.

Thorvaldsen (1770–1844) was the son of a poor Icelandic woodcarver and a Danish mother. He was sent as a boy to the Royal Danish Academy of Fine Arts in Copenhagen, where he won prizes at every stage, culminating in the Great Gold Medal, which came with a travelling scholarship. So in 1797 he went to Rome to learn carving in marble (not readily available in Denmark), rapidly developed a successful practice and ended up staying there for the next 40 years. I had seen him likened to Keats as a humble-born genius who had mastered the educated repertory of classical allusion, but I had seen nothing of the teeming individuality of Keats, the intimacy or originality. I wasn't sure I knew how to look at Thorvaldsen. Could I even tell him apart from Canova, the great contemporary whose death in 1822 left him the most celebrated and sought-after sculptor in Europe?

I guessed that the essential thing, with work of such restraint, was to have plenty of time for it; and this spring I returned for a whole day, starting with a privileged hour before the public was admitted. I would be able to dwell on the sculptures, and return to them in changing aspects, as the shafts of sunlight steepened and slid across them. For nearly a century after its opening in 1848 the Thorvaldsensmuseum was lit only by natural light; in the depths of the northern winter it must have been a most mysterious and sepulchral place, the works emerging from the shadows only for a few hours each day. On a dazzling March morning it promised to come to life.

The city itself, with its wonderful walkable network of old streets and squares and its many towers outdoing each other in fantasy and strangeness, had been turned into a hell of hoardings, barriers, Portakabins, pile-driving and excavations. A new metro was being installed, traffic was diverted, and in the cold early morning the streets were possessed by thousands of cyclists, red-faced in the wind, yelping at any incautious pedestrian who strayed into their lanes. On my way to the museum I warmed up (not quite the right word) at Vor Frue, the cathedral of Copenhagen, designed by the severely neoclassical court architect C. F. Hansen and completed in 1829. The great bare barrel-vaulted nave is lined with Thorvaldsen's monumental figures of the Apostles, but the eye goes at once to the high altar, dominated by his immense bearded Christ, standing with hands stretched out and down to show the stigmata. It still leaves me cold, but I see that the trick of it is to draw the viewer forwards, so as to meet Christ's downcast gaze. Noble and impersonal, it has lent itself to endless reproduction: copies of it adorn Temple Square in Salt Lake City and other Mormon churches across America.

Seen after Hansen's fine but chilly work, the architecture of the Thorvaldsensmuseum seems all the more exhilarating. The building trumpets its own idiosyncrasy. Its 39-year-old architect, M. G. Bindesbøll, had only one previous work to his name, a grain dryer in Norway. Somehow, in competition with far more established figures, for what was to be the first museum in Denmark and a celebration of a national hero, his vibrant novelty won out. The times were changing, and Bindesbøll seems to have been ahead of them. Absolute monarchy in Denmark was to end in 1848, the year the museum opened, and the academic classicism associated with the old order was subverted and reinterpreted in a colourful, eclectic and newly democratic light. Bindesbøll had travelled widely in Greece and Turkey, and his liberated delight in coloured decoration is shown in the drawings he made there, which fed into the vivid decor of the museum.

The temple-like front is as powerful as I remembered, with

five huge splayed doorways, outlined in white against ochre, and tall, pleasingly trapezium-shaped brown doors – a shape repeated in the articulation of all four façades. It is what gives the exterior of this Greco-Roman building its Egyptian look. The magical feature, though, is the two sequences of frescoes by the artist Jørgen Sonne, which run round three sides of the building. They tell the story of the museum itself. In the first strand we see Thorvaldsen's return to Denmark in 1838. Excited crowds gather and wave; in one panel a woman has fallen into the water and is helped back into a boat. Thorvaldsen himself steps ashore in the final panel, to be greeted by various dignitaries and friends, while behind him the mauve-shirted, white-hatted rowers raise their slanting yellow oars in the air. The drawing is lively and clear, and the faces of the unnamed figures typically more strong than handsome, but this side of caricature. The action, all round, unfolds against a black sky, and the boldness of the colour scheme is, oddly, both powerful and charming.

On his return to Copenhagen, the elderly Thorvaldsen announced that he would leave the contents of his Roman studio as well as his own large collections of antiquities and paintings to the nation if a museum were specially built to house them. Around the other two sides we see the arrival of these numerous objects, with the frigate that brought them, anchored along one corner of the building. From it emerge, first of all on rowing boats, and then on primitive wagons and litters, the accumulated spoils of Thorvaldsen's immensely productive career. There are echoes of a Roman triumph, but here the labouring townspeople who are pushing and heaving the trophies are themselves the victors, or at least the beneficiaries, barefoot in accordance with classical precedent, but otherwise in modern breeches, waistcoats and rolled-up sleeves. The Phrygian cap of the kneeling marble Ganymede bobs along beside the red peaked cap of the foreman supervising his transport. The pensively inspired Lord Byron, perched on a broken Grecian column, pen raised to chin, is tended by five men earnestly involved in their own practical task (a sheet caught in a wheel of the truck threatens to be a problem). Noble art works are shown in the care of the common man. His appreciation of them remains a matter of conjecture: an element of latent comedy co-exists with the expression of a tribute. One group of men rest and mop their brows from the effort of pushing Copernicus. Another man with a bust under each arm has a profile to rival either of them. It is hard to convey the simultaneously workaday but momentous, festive but solemn nature of this frieze, which also forms an unusual advertisement for the contents of the museum, "like a sign for a menagerie", as Bindesbøll said, depicting highlights of the show inside.

In the upstairs picture galleries there's a painting by Friedrich Nerly that shows the transportation involved at an earlier stage of the artistic process. A gigantic block of marble, with "Thorvaldsen Roma" marked on it, is dragged along a road from the quarry by a team of six exhausted and collapsing buffaloes. We sense that something superhuman will in due course take place. In another painting we see Pope Leo XII visiting Thorvaldsen's studio, a tiny figure in pink dwarfed by the congregation of immense white sculptures. (The artist appears to be introducing the pope to Jesus Christ.) Thorvaldsen and his team of assistants worked often on a colossal scale. Yet all the largest works in the museum are plaster – usually the original plasters that served as models for the marble, or occasionally bronze, final works, and so fresher and closer to the artist's original vision for all their ambiguous air of being merely copies, or plaster casts. But, being plaster, they have discoloured over their nearly two centuries of existence, from the stove and candle smoke of their days in the Roman studio and from the different pollutants of modern life; they show varying degrees of grubbiness, and many of the smaller busts look as if blackened by incessant handling, though really it seems only by the air. It takes a bit of getting used to, and is shown up all the more by juxtaposition with the sculptures in flawless white marble.

Those giant works call for giant rooms, of which there are two, one of them a church-like space containing the original plasters of *Christ and the Twelve Apostles* where groups of young schoolchildren tend to gather. The other, larger hall was originally the entrance, running the width of the building behind the five great doors, and with its high barrel vault and attic windows it reminds me just a little of the concourse of some very grand neoclassical railway station.

It is dominated at either end by two equestrian figures that seem all the more stunning for their size, each over 15 feet high, and further raised on substantial plinths. On the left Prince Josef Poniatowski rides forward in classical dress, like a supersized Marcus Aurelius, but flourishing a sword rather than the open hand of command. Facing him, Maximilian I, elector of Bavaria, sword sheathed but right hand pointing forward and up, bears down on us magnificently. Poniatowski was designed for Warsaw, Maximilian for Munich. Between them, along the walls, are the seated Copernicus, for Warsaw, and Pope Pius VII, for his tomb monument in St Peter's. It is like some *ad hoc* Pantheon. Thorvaldsen seems to have been unconcerned by the ideology of his subjects or patrons, though the commissioning of a Danish Protestant to do a papal tomb was evidently controversial. The Poniatowski monument suffered repeated vicissitudes, at the hands of Tsar Nicholas I, who wanted it destroyed, and of the Nazis, who blew it to bits when they evacuated Warsaw in 1944. It seems to me both powerful and elusive, because of Thorvaldsen's characteristic way of sublimating the thrilling drama of his subject's end (riding his horse into the River Elster to avoid capture during the Napoleonic retreat) to some more timeless and impersonal image of noble leadership. The original commission had been for Poniatowski to appear in Polish cavalry uniform, the horse rearing before its final jump. Thorvaldsen's quite different conception is impressive and even inspiring, but not a bit dramatic.

It helps to know the stories behind the works, and part of their remoteness to me is due to a patchy classical education. In the long sequences of smaller rooms I am more struck by this distance, and by the rewards of overcoming it. There is a famous *Mercury*, perched on a tree-stump: a fine youthful figure with the perfection of feature and worryingly tiny penis one expects from a neoclassical artist. He has been playing panpipes, now held away from his lips, while his other hand, behind him, has begun to pull his sword from its sheath. I need to be told that he has just charmed Argus to sleep, and is about to kill him. Then the graceful young man in his winged helmet becomes more than picturesque, and I see that Thorvaldsen has chosen a moment, not of drama, but of tense equipoise between two actions. I need, too, to come close and, as with the heroic Christ, meet the downward gaze of the now rather terrifying blank eyes.

The question of how these works were viewed when they were most prized is an interesting one. When the museum first opened, children under confirmation age were not admitted alone for fear of the nudity. In a nearby room there is the superb *Jason with the Golden Fleece*, naked but for sandals and helmet. Eyeing it from across the room is the bust of the wealthy Anglo-Dutch art collector Thomas Hope, who commissioned it, and thus enabled the young Thorvaldsen to stay on in Rome. Thorvaldsen took 25 years to produce the marble figure, which is both a spectacular showpiece and a kind of emblem of his Roman career. Near by are Hope's wife and his two sons. Like many other subjects of busts, Hope tests Thorvaldsen's neoclassical code; what we see of him is conventionally naked (great men, like Byron and Frederick VI, may have togas or sword belts across bare chests) but portraiture still requires a likeness, in this case involving exuberant Regency sideburns. The relationship between Jason and his owner, and his owner's wife and children, has an historical piquancy and even a faint comedy of a kind Thorvaldsen generally prefers us not to see.

Upstairs there are half a dozen portraits of Thorvaldsen himself, which cumulatively show what a lion he was, and prove, rather as pictures of Liszt do, that here was an irresistible subject. He had (the one thing his own sculpted self-portrait cannot convey) the most mesmerising grey eyes, so persistent in portraits from youth to old age that the emphasis on them cannot be mere romantic exaggeration. Indeed, they tend to be rendered with a virtuosic lifelikeness that seems conscious of the distinct responsibilities of paint as opposed to marble. They are the eyes, one realises, as one wanders on from room to room among the things he made and the things he collected, that are the occasion and *sine qua non* of this whole extraordinary place.

Thorvaldsensmuseum
Bertel Thorvaldsens Plads 2, 1213 Copenhagen K, Denmark
www.thorvaldsensmuseum.dk

Palais of the Dolls

MUSÉE DE LA POUPÉE, PARIS

Jacqueline Wilson

The Musée de la Poupée is five minutes' stroll from the Centre Georges Pompidou. You walk away from the bustle and blare of traffic, the squeals and shouting of all the foreign students, the shops selling "I love Paris" T-shirts, and dive down a pretty little alleyway with a sign to the doll museum. It's like stepping straight into a Victorian storybook.

The Musée was started by a father and son, Guido and Samy Odin, determined to find the perfect showcase for their ever-increasing collection of antique dolls. There's the permanent display of 500 dolls in beautiful little tableaux inside glass cabinets, frequently changing themed exhibitions, a room for birthday parties, a doll's hospital and a shop. As Samy Odin admits sadly, all small specialist museums are in a vulnerable position nowadays, and many other doll museums have had to close. But I very much hope the Musée de la Poupée in the Impasse Berthaud stays open for many more decades.

I first went there with my daughter, Emma, nearly 20 years ago. Emma was an adult by then, but we've always shared a love of dolls. When she was little, I frequently took her to Pollock's Toy Museum and the Museum of Childhood in Bethnal Green. I loved to read her Rumer Godden's charming doll stories, and we smiled at Beth's battered dolls in *Little Women* and envied Sara Crewe her magnificent doll, Emily, in *A Little Princess*.

Our family seems always to have been fascinated by dolls. Emma had a large collection throughout her childhood, and was particularly attached to some soft little ragdolls and Sophie, a French doll with a rather vacant expression. My own first doll was a Beauty Skin baby doll called Janet. She started off a pretty pink, but over the years became increasingly jaundiced, though I still loved her dearly. My mother, Biddy, used to take me to see the Christmas dolls in Hamleys and did her best to buy me one every year. We lived in a council flat on very little money and managed without most things (fridge, washing machine, telephone, car), but I was always impeccably dressed and had lovely dolls. Biddy started to collect antique dolls herself, beginning with an Armand Marseille china doll with long hair, bought for ten shillings from a junk shop. As a small girl I combed this poor doll's hair so frequently that she developed alopecia and had to wear a sun bonnet to hide her bald patches.

My grandmother Hilda Ellen loved dolls too and had a magnificent large German china doll called Mabel. Hilda Ellen had few other toys. She was rather like the little waifs and strays I write about, a motherless child farmed out to various unsuitable relations from the age of seven. I loved to hear her tell stories about her early life. When my great-grandfather married again and had two small children by his new wife, he brought the teenage Hilda Ellen back into the family home to act as an unpaid nursemaid. She had been given the beautiful china doll one Christmas by a local charity and it was still her most treasured possession, even if she was now too old to play with it.

My great-grandfather was a wheeler-dealer, ever the opportunist. It was wartime and new German dolls were obviously not available. He decided to set up his own doll factory with a colleague. He didn't have the faintest idea how to make dolls, so despite Hilda Ellen's protests he decapitated and dismembered Mabel to see how she was constructed.

I suppose Mabel didn't die in vain, because my great-grandfather's doll-manufacturing business, Nunn & Smeed, was reasonably successful from 1915 to 1927. They didn't just use Mabel as a prototype. They went on to invent their own special walking doll with spring hinges at the knees. There's a photograph of this not particularly attractive doll "walking" jauntily in *Pollock's Dictionary of English Dolls*.

She can't hold a candle to her beautiful French sisters in the Musée de la Poupée. Emma and I go to see them every year when we're in Paris. It's our little nostalgic treat. It's clearly a special outing for many mothers and daughters. The child visitors to the museum all seem too good to be true – polite, quiet little girls with Alice bands and pinafore dresses and snowy white socks, gazing intently at each glass cabinet and whispering intelligent questions.

Samy Odin told me that he's hoping to be able to refurbish his museum next year, but I rather hope it stays just as it is, crammed to bursting point, with doll's prams and furniture balanced on top of the cabinets. The first thing you see when you go into the museum is a very large doll's house with 20 small dolls in various costumes: a sailor suit, a Scottish outfit, a Breton costume, a First Holy Communion dress, even a jolly jester party frock. These are all clothes made from patterns in a magazine, *La Semaine de Suzette*, featuring a very popular little doll, Bleuette. The Bleuettes have bisque heads and are under a foot in height, cheery little creatures displayed in their own fully furnished house. There's even a tiny feather duster so they can keep their rooms spick and span.

It's easy to stare at them so long that you feel sucked into their own perfect little world. The loudly ticking clock in the hushed museum makes you especially aware that for a very modest tariff you're taking a step back in time. This sense of time travel is increased when you see the only modern dolls in the permanent collection, portrait dolls by Catherine Dève, lovingly copied from family photographs of Samy Odin as a little boy, his mother, Vera, as a child, and his grandmother Madeleine, all aged about five and playing together happily with their toys.

Vera died when Samy was little, and Guido brought him up single-handedly. He had a photography studio in a village in the Italian Alps and took many photographs of women in their traditional costumes. He displayed his photographs imaginatively, with costumes and dressed dolls. Guido was given an old broken doll to mend, and the teenage Samy was fascinated. Guido gave Samy an English book about dolls for his birthday, thinking it would help him learn the language. They both became passionately interested and started collecting.

Samy studied literature and became a teacher while Guido continued with photography and theatrical costume design. His sewing skills were a tremendous bonus when an antique doll needed a new outfit. They started to exhibit their dolls, and in 1994 founded the Musée de la Poupée. Both men continue to collect and attend doll conventions all over the world. Samy has written numerous books about dolls – and touchingly has dedicated his major work, *Fascinating Dolls*, to "Guido Odin, my father, who made this amazing adventure possible".

The Odins' collection is wide and varied, and the exhibits are arranged painstakingly to delight and instruct children. There's one cabinet showing that dolls can be used for all different purposes, even as representations of celebrities. I love the dapper Maurice Chevalier doll, stockinette over cardboard, with a very lifelike painted face and removable clothes – though it seems an impertinence to imagine little Maurice stripped down to his underwear. There's also an insistently pink pyjama-case dolly beside a beautiful 1870s fortune-teller doll with a swivel head and a wide skirt made up of numerous folded paper fortunes. There are wooden dolls, porcelain, wax, leather, papier-mâché, celluloid, rubber, and little delicate paper dolls miraculously untorn and preserved intact for 150 years. There are china dolls as big as children, and tiny little dolls the size of a thumb. These pocket dolls were sold by La Poupée Modèle and called Mignonnette. Little girls could make extensive wardrobes for them. My favourite is a bizarre Eiffel Tower outfit: the little Mignonnette wears a pink dress decorated with silver braid stamped with the date 1889, and sports a miniature Eiffel Tower on her auburn curls like a droll hat.

The 19th-century lady dolls are all exquisitely dressed, often with little reticules and parasols and tiny kid gloves and minute fans and opera glasses. One very splendid 1860s Steiner doll wears a black and pale-green silk dress and is clearly well into her teens, but she says "Papa, Maman" like a toddler as she raises her arms and "waltzes" to left and right. Her mechanism is still in good working order and her pale blue eyes and blonde hair are immaculate because she was only taken out of her box and played with one day each year by her original owners.

Infant dolls are displayed amusingly, 15 babies of varying sizes in the care of two adult dolls. One is a nursemaid in a costume specially made by Guido, the other is a magnificent fairy queen with a bisque head by Simon & Halbig. She has a bejewelled head-dress and a pearl-trimmed silk frock and two very long blonde plaits. She looks capable of charming all the babies and effort-lessly keeping them quiet but, just in case, one nursing doll has his mouth stoppered by a wooden dummy.

There are more babies in an enormous seaside tableau, a disconcertingly large assembly of naked celluloid dolls making sandcastles in front of a painted sea. There's a magnificent array of plastic picnicware laid out beside them – but no food! There's also a school display of character babies, one screaming his head off, another wearing a dunce's cap, each sitting at a wooden desk with authentic little ink splotches.

These detailed displays delight small visitors – but this is also a museum to interest serious doll collectors. The Odins are particularly proud of their Jumeau *bébés*. These aren't actual infant dolls; they are little girl (and occasionally little boy) dolls, exquisitely made, with beautiful expressions. The Jumeau dollmaking firm was founded in the early 1840s by Pierre François Jumeau, and his son Emile developed the business so that the beautiful dolls were much prized throughout the 1870s, 1880s and 1890s. The heads were made of fine kaolin paste, moulded in plaster casts, then carefully painted pale pink. Their eyes were wonderfully realistic, painstakingly made from coloured glass rods. Jumeau insisted his factory workers served a long apprenticeship to become proficient and employed little orphan girls so that they had a chance to learn a trade.

Samy's favourite is the Premier Portrait Jumeau, one of the first series produced in the late 1870s. She's 25 inches high, very pale and delicate, with beautiful blue eyes and dark gold curls. She's wearing immaculate original clothing, a red lace-trimmed dress with a tiny Kate Greenaway pattern, white polka-dot stockings and black leather tied shoes. She even has tiny black jet earrings. He also admires a little ten-and-a-half-inch blonde *bébé* in a cream dress with brown velvet ribbon and blue leather shoes to match her eyes. Both dolls were kept and cherished by the families of the original owners, and were clearly only played with on very special occasions.

Jumeau *bébés* can have closed or open mouths with little pearly teeth. There is a very large 1890s open-mouthed doll in the collection in a magnificent pale pink bonnet and silk dress. She's smiling sweetly but her expression is a little disconcerting because she has very pronounced Frida Kahlo eyebrows. My favourites are the *bébés tristes* – they translate as long-faced Jumeau babies, the dolls having distinctive wistful expressions. There's a very fancy example in beautiful condition, wearing a green and red sailor costume with a saucy red straw hat, but the largest *bébé*, at 30 inches, is the one I like best. She's got long blonde curls and big brown eyes, and she wears a pale green silk hat with a satin rose and a matching dress abundantly edged with cream lace. Guido and Samy bid for her in a public sale, and when they made the clinching offer they were applauded by the whole room.

Not all their dolls are on display at one time. Samy and Guido have a remarkable private collection of dolls with extensive wardrobes. I've seen photographs of a pair of Jumeau *bébés*, Charlotte and Suzanne, with striking sky-blue eyes. They were originally owned by two sisters, Claire and Pauline, who each received a magnificent Jumeau doll on their 11th birthday. Imagine giving a doll to an 11-year-old now! But Claire and Pauline clearly played elaborate games with their dolls, dressing them up in velvet coats with matching hats, serving them many little meals on their own tiny china dinner service. I'm sure they enjoyed getting them ready for bed, using their own little washstand and possibly the miniature china chamber pot.

Many of the dolls in the museum have little dogs or teddy bears to play with. There's a small Steiff bear that looks as if he's been through the wars. He has a distinctly melancholy expression, and one arm and one leg are carefully bandaged. He was donated by Edith Coisson, who ran an orphanage in Italy. She'd give each new orphan the little bear for comfort – until the next orphan arrived. Maybe the bear got his injuries from a tug-of-war between two children.

There were some 1920s and 1930s Lenci cloth dolls on display when Emma and I visited, and I found them a little alarming. Their very rouged cheeks, red pouty lips and ultra-curly hair reminded me of those terrifying tots in American beauty pageants. By contrast, we greeted the more modern dolls as if they were old friends: there were the Holly Hobbies that used to be crammed into Emma's doll's cot, and the exact twin of her little Sophie doll, a *poupée*, with no mouth, big black button eyes and very long fair hair. There was even a set of Emma's 1960s Sindies looking like a miniature cast of *Mad Men*.

I think this is part of the charm of toy museums – to have that little thrill of recognition. It had an added resonance for me, because my glamorous professional daughter suddenly became that long-ago little girl with a pageboy haircut and stripy dungarees, begging me to play dolls with her.

It's hard to explain precisely the charm of dolls. Balzac kept a little collection of doll's house dolls on his desk and said they helped him invent his fictional characters, but some people find their intense glassy gaze disconcerting and recoil from their little outstretched fingers. I find them enchanting. I don't often give them to the children in my own books because most girls hide away from them by the time they start junior school. My latest book, however, has a solemn old-fashioned child narrator called Rosalind. In one chapter she goes back to Edwardian times to meet E. Nesbit's characters, and she has a wonderful time in their nursery, playing with their china dolls.

Musée de la Poupée
7 Impasse Berthaud, 75003 Paris, France
www.museedelapoupeeparis.com

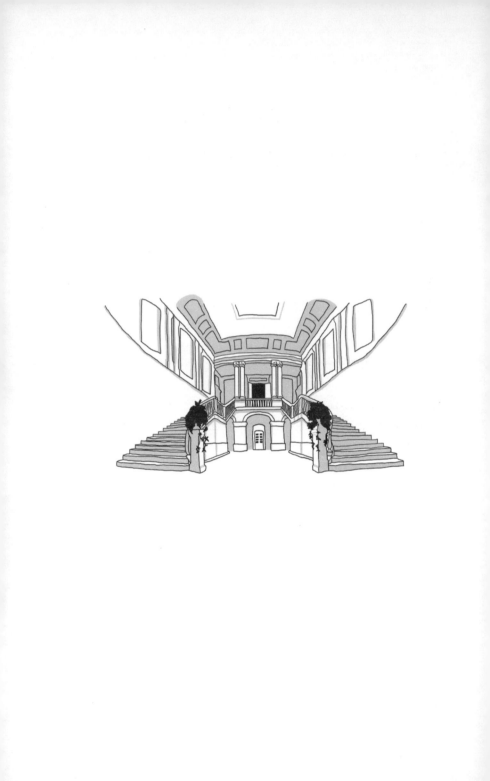

The Odessaphiles

ODESSA STATE LITERARY MUSEUM, ODESSA

A. D. Miller

Perhaps it's the influence of his stories, with their subtle narrators and exquisite understatement, but to me the smiles on Isaac Babel's face in the black-and-white photographs in the Odessa State Literary Museum all seem ironic. It's hard, too, knowing a little about his life and how it ended, not to suspect that one of the ironies Babel might have been contemplating was the transience of success, even the violence that might one day supersede the accolades the Stalinist state had heaped upon him. Looking at the wiry spectacles pinned to the wall, I think of the pair that must have perched on the pale, fragile dome of Babel's head when the secret police took him to the Lubyanka.

Babel is Odessa's best-known literary son. But this wonderful museum, housed in a pale-blue tsarist-era palace, isn't devoted only to Odessa's own, or to its magical and dreadful history, though it encompasses both. Because of its location – on the Black Sea, at what was the Russian and then the Soviet empire's sunny southern limit – many of those empires' greatest authors were exiled to Odessa, fled through its docks or came here for their health or a debauch. Embracing the transients and flâneurs, this is, in effect, a museum of Russian literature. And, being Russian, it becomes a museum of censorship and repression as well as art: of genius and bravery, blood and lies.

*

There are lots of museums devoted to famous writers, but fewer dedicated purely to literature. This one was conceived and founded by Nikita Brygin, a bibliophile and ex-KGB officer. He left the KGB in murky circumstances, but remained sufficiently well connected to secure a handsome venue near the sea for his eccentric scheme – the ceilings are cracking, but the chandeliers and reliefs conjure the mood of the aristocratic balls for which the palace was built. He sent a team of young women across the Soviet Union to secure writerly artefacts for the collection, which is arranged in a suite of bright first-floor rooms reached by a grand double staircase. Opened in 1984, the museum survived Odessa's transition from the defunct Soviet Union to independent Ukraine. Today, it is overseen by elderly attendants whose sternness yields to solicitous enthusiasm when one of their infrequent visitors approaches. The place runs on love.

For me, this is a memento of the years I spent travelling across the former Soviet Union as a foreign correspondent – the most exhilarating, frustrating, sad and privileged years of my life. I loved both Odessa and the museum when I first came in 2006, but the stories I wrote on that trip were bleak ones, about smuggling through the port and sex trafficking through the ferry terminal. A woman from a charity that helps victims of trafficking told me how to spot them among the passengers disembarking the ships from Istanbul: hungry, hangdog expressions; no luggage; clothes ill suited to the season. The sex trade is the dark side of the licence and loucheness for which Odessa has always been renowned.

Pushkin is partly to blame for the city's raunchy reputation. In the margins of the manuscripts of *Eugene Onegin*, which he started writing in Odessa, he doodled portraits of some of the women he slept with here. Facsimiles, complete with lavish crossings-out, are on view in the museum. You look at the sketches and think of the young poet, bored by his own genius. Legend has it that, exiled from St Petersburg by the tsar, Pushkin began an affair with Countess Vorontsova, the wife of Odessa's governor. Another of his local flames, Karolina Sobanska, was also the sometime lover of Adam Mickiewicz (a cherished Polish poet commemorated in the museum) and a long-term spy for the tsarist secret police. Count Vorontsov, the peeved governor, dispatched Pushkin to write a report about a locust infestation, before running him permanently out of town.

You can still sense Odessa's erotic tension and potential in its balmy *passeggiata* and suggestively latticed balconies. In my novel *Snowdrops*, mostly set in Moscow, I send the narrator, Nick Platt, down to Odessa as the dénouement approaches. Nick is a chronic self-deluder and a man of fatally easy virtue. Here, he says, "you can somehow make things seem better than they truly are. You can make things be what you want them to be." Odessa, a breeding ground for fabulists, seemed the right place for him.

Yet, like many ports, Odessa stands for freedom as well as sleaze. Revolutionaries and their ideas have been smuggled in and out along with contraband goods. Each of the museum's rooms represents a period in the city's intellectual history, evoking a particular era through furniture and design, and often concentrating on a characteristic genre. In the room depicting the 1850s and 1860s, there is a run of issues of *The Bell*, the journal published by Alexander Herzen during his London exile, which was sneaked into Russia through Odessa's docks.

Freedom, in fact, was the point of Odessa. Founded by Catherine the Great in 1794 as a free port, it soon became probably the most cosmopolitan city in the world, drawing in Greeks, Poles, Germans, Italians, Tatars, Turks, Armenians, runaway serfs and Jews fleeing the anti-Semitic restrictions in force across the rest

of the Russian empire. Even today, with its Mediterranean architecture and post-Soviet ricketiness, Odessa seems to belong to
many other places, and at the same time only to itself. Poetry and
polemic in a variety of languages, forgotten heroes of foreign
struggles and minority masterpieces are remembered in the
museum's portraits and manuscripts.

At the opposite end of the empire from St Petersburg, warm
where the former capital is chilly, Odessa is its opposite in other
ways too. Whereas St Petersburg is a "premeditated city", as Dostoyevsky put it, built by Peter the Great on the blood and bones of
slaves, Odessa grew up spontaneously on commerce.

The blood came later. At the turn of the 20th century the
region was overtaken by pogroms and then the Russian revolution. Anyone inclined to believe that revolutions are chiefly
a pretext for bloodletting and score-settling will find that view
amply corroborated in *Cursed Days*, Ivan Bunin's diary of life in
the city during the Russian civil war. In the museum you can sit
at the dressing table rescued from Bunin's rooms and see yourself
in his mirror, wondering, perhaps, how you might have coped,
what compromises you might have made, in the chaos of rumour
and mob thuggery that *Cursed Days* describes. The mirror is half
patched with letters and family photographs, and the remaining, exposed glass is mottled. The blotches aren't blood, but they
make you think of blood.

Revolutionary Odessa, Bunin writes, was "a dead, burned-
out city", a nightmare place stalked by tramps and drunks armed
with revolvers and cutlasses. His is a more reliable account of
revolutionary upheaval than Sergei Eisenstein's brilliant but
wildly mendacious *Battleship Potemkin*, a propaganda version of
a naval mutiny in 1905. The film has a famous scene of a pram
careening down the steps from Odessa's seafront boulevard to

the water. A cartoon sketch of Eisenstein and a poster advertising the film's release appear in a room that deals with the cinema and drama of the 1920s. These days, visitors who stroll along from the museum to the "Potemkin Steps" can have themselves photographed with an impressive array of exotic animals, for a small consideration.

Exhausted by fear and depravity, Bunin caught the last boat out of Odessa with the retreating French forces in 1920. When, a few years later, Isaac Babel published his *Odessa Tales*, one of the cycles of short stories that made his reputation, the milieu they portrayed had already been swallowed by strife.

They all came to Odessa – all the classic Russian writers I have learned to revere. Gogol came south for his health. There is a sort of shrine to him in the museum, in a shadowy alcove formed by a dark, cruciform bookshelf and an ornate, frieze-covered wall. Chekhov passed through, on his way to and from the penal colony of Sakhalin Island, and so did Tolstoy: the young writer in one of the photographs in the collection looks a lifetime away from the iconically bearded sage. At least, almost all of them came. The notable exception is Dostoyevsky, who never visited Odessa – which may explain a lot.

The Soviet-era masters too. Anna Akhmatova was born here. Mayakovsky fell in love in Odessa, as one of his poems records: "It happened. It happened in Odessa ..." His mad visage stares from a photo in the museum, appearing as the 19th-century style of the earlier galleries gives way to constructivist patterns, slanting collages and striking red frames that signify the great disjuncture. In the lovely, lush statue garden that runs along one of the walls, abode of dead writers and live cats, there is a monument to Vladimir Vysotsky, a hell-raising Russian *chanteur* and one of the

Soviet Union's finest poets. Vysotsky was also an actor; he made films in Odessa's studios, and sang about a longing to come here. If I could go back in time to attend any gig, I would choose one of Vysotsky's semi-clandestine performances in the 1970s.

Still, for me, Babel, born in Odessa in 1894, is the presiding genius. It's partly the Jewish connection, which adds another layer of darkness and light to the Odessa story. My first book was about my Jewish forebears' emigration from what was then Galicia and is now western Ukraine, to the East End of London at the end of the 19th century. Anyone researching Jewish life in that region at that time encounters the legend of old Odessa. Once among the great Jewish cities of Europe, it was a sort of seedier, commercial version of fin-de-siècle Vienna: an incubator of self-confident, enlightened Jews, where opera and cantorial music mingled, and Jewish families sent violinists and chancers out into the world in roughly equal measure. In early 20th-century London, I discovered, there was a fearsome Jewish gang called the Odessans.

Then I read Babel's *Odessa Tales*, colourful early editions of which are mounted alongside the photographs of him in the museum. The tales feature women who wear scented lingerie, flap black fans and stake gold coins; and they star Benya Krik – Benya the King – the leader of Odessa's Jewish gangsters. Benya burns down the police station on the night of his sister's wedding. "Everyone makes mistakes, even God," he tells a mother whose son has just been shot by one of his henchmen. When you've had enough of Odessa's palaces, you can take a tour of the Moldavanka, Benya's neighbourhood, and peer into its courtyards, now populated by defeated dogs, noisy children, men working on ancient cars, and young women stepping out of hovels but looking like $2 million.

So I was primed to admire Babel by my background, but also,

I think, by the pattern of my career. Babel, for me, is the supreme journalist-turned-fiction-writer. Serving as a correspondent during the Polish-Soviet war of 1920, he rode into battle with the Cossack cavalry, improbable company for a Jewish intellectual. Afterwards he transmuted those experiences into *Red Cavalry*, the collection of quietly appalled war stories that are his finest achievement. He published very little after these, riskily referring to himself as a "master of the genre of silence". But he stayed in the Soviet Union when he might have defected: a classic, passive Russian heroism.

Babel was shot in 1940, around the same time as several lesser writers mentioned in the museum, some of whom might have gone on to be as distinguished as he was. Not long afterwards Jewish Odessa was destroyed in violence that, even by the standards of the second world war, is difficult to read about. The war and its cultural impact are discussed in a set of rooms on the museum's ground floor. There are blown-up photos of ruined streets and liberating Soviet soldiers; also, less conspicuously, preserved orders from the Romanian occupiers for Jews to assemble and ghettoise. Like many Jews, when I look at these blandly genocidal documents I have a dim, irrational sense that this could have been me and mine.

In a way there is surprisingly little about Babel in the museum. But perhaps this is as it should be. The exhibition has remained largely unchanged since the 1980s. By then Babel had been rehabilitated, but he wasn't quite a whole person again; nor was the whole truth about Soviet crimes accepted and circulated. The displays are coy about the fates of some of the writers they mention. The photos of Babel do not include the haggard mug shots taken after his arrest.

And so, in a mild form, the museum is itself an example of the censorship that both thwarted and stimulated its subjects. Nikita Brygin, its founder, knew that about his project from first-hand experience. Party bosses, reputedly nervous about the enlightened atmosphere Brygin was creating, forced him out of the museum before it opened. He died in 1985 without ever seeing the finished article. Even without his final guidance, the exhibition is in some ways daring for its time, both in design and content. But it remains an artefact of its era. Perhaps that makes it even more valuable. Like the city, the history and the culture it celebrates, it is a glorious achievement with an underside.

The years I spent in Russia broadened my literary and moral horizons. And they made me think about the relationship between the two: between art and the suffering that sometimes seems to gestate it. Odessa has been a theatre of both art and suffering, and the museum is a testament to that synergy. I love the city, the museum and Russian literature; but, in the end, they aren't and couldn't be worth it. They aren't worth all the blood that has gone into them.

Odessa State Literary Museum
2 Lanzheronovskaya Street, Odessa 65026, Ukraine
www.odessatourism.org/en/do/museums/literary-museum

A Smiling Shrunken Goddess

CORINIUM MUSEUM, CIRENCESTER

Alice Oswald

When I was six, I went on a school trip to a museum. I don't know where it was. I can remember only a set of steps leading round a corner. I ran down the steps and came face to face with an orang-utan. I wasn't sure whether it was alive, but I shouted at the top of my voice and Mrs Copestakes told me off: first for running, second for shouting and third for pronouncing it "orange you-tang". There's nothing else I remember about the place, just the steps and the gingery tall creature (the first corpse I ever saw) looking down at me.

Since then, I haven't been to many museums. I can't help being depressed by the aloofness of things behind glass. There seems to be always such a dead weight of description of what is really just a long tradition (and I'm part of it) of eating and cleaning and killing and decaying.

But a few years ago, I stepped into the Corinium Museum in Cirencester. It had been recently refurbished, so that alongside its objects I found various waxwork people in Roman clothes. Corinium was an important Roman town and there (still there) was its butcher, stuck to his cleaver, hovering over a dead chicken; a soldier, depressed and paralysed on his bunk; a family of four at odds with each other in a sitting room. Upstairs, there were graves which started grumbling when I touched a screen: "Ah, citizen! I know what you're thinking! How did one of the locals gain so much wealth? I put those hooded cloaks on the map. Just the thing in this dreadful climate …" And here and there, under huge floating paragraphs on red boards, and looking rather pale by contrast, there were things that had been touched by Romans: a buckle, a handle, a strainer, seven copper-alloy and silver spoons, coins, pots, weights, probes, a surgical hook, a pillar, a plough.

It's very hard to look at things. Here I am, sitting in my shed remembering the Romans, not really noticing the hard-worked figure of my biro pushing at the page. I could pause and note down its yellowness, its inky beak, its self-reliant but friendly, exhausted way of leaning on the forefinger, but it would seem pedantic and anyway the pen would simply go on being densely itself alongside my adjectives. It's the same with spoons and hooks and buckles. All day my hands understand them, but my attention is some-where else, normally a few hours behind or ahead of what I'm doing. The fact is, it's impossible (except by accident) to imagine the present, which is why it's so frustrating trying to imagine the past.

So I stepped into the Corinium Museum and I was wafting around the place, filling up with facts and exchanging the occa-sional glance with a paralysed butcher or soldier, not really looking at anything (at least not in the fleeting and practical way it would like to be looked at), when I came across a water nymph. She was perhaps 30 times smaller than an orang-utan but every bit as compelling.

Just to put this in context, it was 2005: the year we moved from Devon to Gloucestershire. In Devon, we'd been living by the Dart, which is a 52-mile river of the kind that drowns people: as wide as a motorway and in places about 20 feet deep. In our part of Gloucestershire, the closest river was the Dunt, a runnel no deeper than my boots, a mere glint in a field, mostly lost in nettles. For the first month after moving, that whole landscape made me thirsty, not just with a throat thirst, but with a thirst of the eyes and the ears; which is why I recognised instantly this 2-inch creature of water sealed behind glass.

She had no accompanying information, only a number and a footnote saying "Roman bone figure of a water nymph", so I had no option but to look at her very hard. What I saw was an Iron-Age, slightly damaged pocket goddess, with left arm and both lower legs missing. She had tool marks on the breast. She was smiling, looking outwards, pouring water from a spilling vase held lightly under a long-fingered hand. Her shoulders had sheen but not shine. She seemed off-guard, in charge of water but not much concerned, curved like an old moon or question mark, crippled but making light of it, no clothes, even her flesh made of bone (whose bone?), very slim, as if her weight had been worn down by water but there was no water anywhere near her. Even the little slurp tipping from her vase was made of a bone and as dry as a bone.

A nymph is a shrunken goddess, a local land-spirit displaced by bigger, more abstract forces. This one took her form from Greece, her refinement from Rome, her material from Britain and was probably made by a Gloucestershire craftsman, working for a Roman, trying to give him power over a Gloucestershire river – perhaps the Churn, which flows through Cirencester, or the Dunt, which flows into the Churn.

In classical mythology, rivers are male but their sources female, or at least attended by females. The source of the Dunt is attended by brambles, hazels, elderflower and nettles. It has two stone ledges where a farmer could, if he wished, place a bone figure of a water nymph. Or he could leave her at his household shrine among other miniature gods and pray to her each morning. Or he could carry her in his pocket (apparently togas did have pockets) so that he could stand around talking while his hands kept in touch with water; just as some people jingle loose change while they're talking, to keep the conversation profitable.

"In Java," according to Frazer's *Golden Bough* (1922 edition),

> two men will sometimes thrash each other with supple rods till the blood flows down their backs … in some parts of southern and western Russia … after service in church the priest in his robes has been thrown down on the ground and drenched with water by his parishioners … in 1868 the prospect of a bad harvest, caused by a prolonged drought induced the inhabitants of a village in the Tarashchansk district to dig up the body of a dissenter, who had died in the preceding December. Some of the party beat the corpse or what was left of it about the head, exclaiming "give us rain!" while others poured water on it through a sieve.

I admire these extreme ways of invoking rain, just as I admire anyone who dares, by means of metaphor (and all language is rooted in metaphor), to communicate with something that isn't human. If you've paid money for seeds or animals and you want to increase their worth by growing them on, then a water nymph is not some kind of a literary personification of water, nor is it a liquefaction of women, but it's an effort, driven by absolute need, to make contact with something inscrutable. It goes without saying that water, because it is transparent and therefore only partially itself, is even more inscrutable than a buckle or a biro – and far more necessary.

I spent a couple of hours looking at the water nymph and bought a postcard in order to keep looking at her. Then I drove home, and when I rounded the last corner into the Dunt valley, it had changed. The river was still small, but the energy of its water was visible everywhere: a kind of downward suction, like a long inhalation of the sea drawing everything towards it. What had happened, I suppose, was that the water nymph (like the orang-utan) had brought me back to the present. It had updated my imagination – and that, as far as I'm concerned, is the main function of the past and the true value of museums.

That all took place seven years ago, but when I was asked to write this article, my first thought was YES if I can HOLD the water nymph. I should perhaps have remembered the story of Actaeon, the huntsman who came upon Diana bathing with her nymphs in a woodland pool. Diana, enraged, turned him into a stag and he was eaten by his own dogs. You should never look too closely at a nymph or goddess.

Well, I was allowed, thanks to the generosity of the Corinium Museum, to put on white gloves and hold the water nymph. She lay very light in the pool of my hand but I couldn't really see her. I couldn't concentrate. Having released her from her glass prison, I now found myself stuck in the glass prison of a camera lens, being looked at looking at a nymph. So there I was, sealed into photographic paper, just noticing the smile on the water nymph's face – not so much the fleeting, bashful smile of a local river – more like the bone-dry smirk of an enraged goddess.

Corinium Museum
Park Street, Cirencester, Gloucestershire GL7 2BX, UK
www.coriniummuseum.org

Sons and Mothers

ENSORHUIS, OSTEND

John Burnside

In 1976, when I was home from Cambridge Tech on Easter vacation, my mother announced, to my father's dismay, that she wanted to "go abroad" in the summer. At first, thinking myself firmly on the sidelines, I encouraged the idea: at 46, Mum had never been farther from home in the East Midlands than Blackpool, and I thought a trip would do her good. I also liked any plan that might discomfit my father, with whom I'd spent most of my teens feuding. It was only two days later, when she added that this holiday might also serve as my graduation present, that I balked: I hadn't been away with the family since a disastrous fortnight at a Clacton holiday camp six years earlier, which I spent wandering the seafront in the small hours, unable to sleep for my father's epic snoring (by day, I napped in the camp cinema, where they played *Doctor Who and the Daleks* every afternoon). By now, though, it was too late to backtrack and, a few months later, we found ourselves, my parents, my younger sister and I, on the ferry to Ostend.

I have no idea why my mother wanted to go there – all she would say was that it sounded nice in the brochure – but with the die irretrievably cast, I resolved to play the good son, taking part, and being one of the family. However, thanks to my father, those good resolutions didn't last and, apart from a couple of excruciating coach tours to Ghent and Sluis, I spent much of that holiday wandering the narrow streets around Ostend's main square, where, among other attractions, I found a surprisingly good Museum of Fine Arts, now rehoused at Mu.ZEE, on Romestraat. That in turn led me to the tall, thin house on Vlaanderenstraat where the painter, musician and occasional writer James Ensor had lived and worked. He was there from 1917, when he inherited the property from an aunt, until his death at the age of 89 in 1949. By then, Ensor was no longer the scandalous figure he had been back in the 1880s. There are those who claim that his later work shows evidence of a slackening-off, of decline even, but I beg to differ. The paintings he made at the Vlaanderenstraat house were certainly quieter, but they have a philosophical depth, and an insight into space and time, that sets them squarely in the oeuvre as valuable works by a major artist.

From the street, the Ensorhuis didn't look like much, but the moment I walked through the door, I was hooked. I even tried to get my mother to visit, but she said it didn't sound like her kind of thing, and I had to agree. I had come to see that nothing I liked was her kind of thing and it saddened me that we had so little in common.

Now, returning to the Ensorhuis, I am struck by how little it has changed. The ground floor still harks back to pre-Ensor days, when it was his Uncle Leopold's shell and souvenir shop. (Ensor's parents also owned a chain of souvenir outlets, importing shells, Oriental vases, semi-precious stones and masks for the annual carnival celebrations which James would re-imagine, sometimes as deeply sinister images, throughout his career.) Perhaps the most interesting exhibits here are the Fiji mermaids, bizarre curiosities made by grafting the head and forearms of a monkey onto the body of a fish, but the whole room is a spectacular jumble of carnival masks, marine life, mannequin heads, Japanese fans, exotic seashells and ghostly corals, a kind of surreal Wunderkammer that seems less deliberately contrived than a matter of natural serendipity. Yet fascinating as this lower level is, what matters to me now is the upper floor, where Ensor created the extraordinary paintings that, the moment I saw them, back in the 1970s, became a permanent part of my inner landscape.

What attracts me most is the variety of the work. Ensor is renowned for his nightmarish, sometimes scatological images of the Belgian carnival, in which he himself would appear as a Christ figure being mocked by the crowd (which included fellow artists and politicians). Yet, throughout his career, he also created quiet meditative works on transience and *le néant* (nothingness), from *The Bathing Hut. Afternoon, July 29, 1876*, through the *Still Life with Blue Pitcher* of 1891 to the late seascapes and interiors. At the same time, the grotesque spirit of *Skeletons Fighting over a Pickled Herring* (1891) recurs in the strangest places, as in the seemingly routine portrait of a lady who, when she refused to pay his fee, found herself transformed into a buck-toothed, pockmarked crone.

That no original works are kept at the Ensorhuis is not important. (The pictures that line the Blue Salon, which also houses Ensor's harmonium, are high-quality reproductions, but the originals are elsewhere, in national galleries all over the world.) What matters is the sense of the man himself that this house provides, a sense that, for me, is wonderfully contradictory. Here was a self-proclaimed anarchist who, during the course of a seemingly polite bourgeois existence, in a polite seaside resort, created some of the most unsettling works of the early 20th century – works that, foreshadowing Surrealism, and Dada, were considered deeply scandalous in his youth and even, on occasion, banned. It comes as no surprise that Ensor, in an address to Albert Einstein in 1933, would say, "Let us justly appreciate the old opportune Belgian motto: Light bursts forth from the collision of ideas", for, like Einstein, Ensor himself was a happy bundle of contradictions and collisions. His art reveals the constant interplay between complementary forces that, moment by moment, gives rise to a present order and, at the same time, exposes any permanent condition we might impose upon the real as temporary and provisional, a mask for the time being that, more often than not, is the most we can hope for.

The strange thing about going back to a place is that, no matter how familiar it may look, something is missing. For me, at the Ensorhuis, it is the masks: yes, the house is full of them but, over the years, my imagination has added hundreds more, masks I have gathered from Ensor's work, carnival masks I have seen elsewhere, masks with no connection to Ensor, all pulled in from memory and compiled to make my own version of the house in which the stairwells are deeper, the hallways wider and higher, every wall a sea of plaster and papier-mâché and shellac faces. Certainly, what appealed to me back then was that mask collection – and my reasons may have been more personal than I realised. Masks conceal, but they can also slip, and each slip brings a new surprise. Clearly, there has always been something unknown behind the façade, but when we do catch a glimpse of that other, hidden face, it is often very different from what we assumed, or hoped for, or feared. At the same time, revelation is a two-way process. According to Ensor, "vision alters while it observes", and this is especially true when, having been granted a chance glimpse of what was once hidden, we are surprised, and altered, by finding that what we see is a far cry from what we had imagined. At such times, it's not just that a secret has been laid open to view, it's that our way of seeing changes, opening onto a wholly other world, familiar in some ways, vitally different in others.

I see, now, how personal all this had become back in 1976, because it was during our holiday in Ostend that I first saw past the mask my mother kept for me. Of course, I knew her life was full of disappointments, but until then I hadn't quite recognised that I was one of them. I may have gained a degree from an obscure technical college (a college I'd attended because I couldn't think of anything else to do), but by that summer it was clear that I had no ambitions, no prospects and no overall plan, other than to avoid being part of "the system". By that summer, I was no longer the gifted son, destined for the successful life my mother had begun to hope for when the teachers at one school after another remarked that I was a clever child, a boy who could go on to great things, a boy, one said, who could do "anything". She had been fed those stories right up to the point when I got expelled from Pope John XXIII Comprehensive in Corby and, even after that, she had thought I would return to the fold, if not as a gold-medal-winning physicist like my cousin John, then at least as a teacher, like my Aunt Eleanor, or a civil servant, like Uncle Tom. But that summer even those more modest successes must have seemed remote – and one afternoon over tea and cakes in the hotel lobby, with my sister upstairs in her room and my father off in a bar somewhere, she asked me straight out what I planned to do with my life. It was the question my father frequently taunted me with, but she had never asked it before. Now, suddenly, she did – and I had no answer.

"Those things don't matter to me," I said, aware of how lame I sounded.

She pursed her lips. "Well, then. What does?"

I didn't say anything – and it was then that I saw how hurt she was, not just by my father's drinking and general unreliability, or by the injustices of a class system that kept people like her down all their lives, but by what she saw as my failure. It must have seemed a perverse failure, too, because I had a degree and that should have counted for something. But I didn't give a damn about the degree, and I didn't give a damn about success or failure, either.

"So what are you going to do?" she said. "If you don't watch out, you'll end up at the Works, like your father. Or in a factory, like me and your sister."

"Well," I said. "What's wrong with that?"

She didn't say anything then, she just sat staring at me in disbelief, no doubt wondering what had happened to make me so indifferent. Instead of reassuring her, I found myself closing down, turning inward, refusing even to acknowledge her concerns. What was the point, anyway? We were family, yes, but we occupied entirely separate worlds and I wasn't going to jump through the usual hoops so she could tell my aunts and cousins how proud she was of me. I don't know if she saw this in my face, or if she was simply at the end of a long process of giving up on me (and from that moment on, I think she did give up, though she loved me to the end), but whatever the reason, she just went upstairs to her room. We didn't say another word about it, ever again.

There is a painting of Ensor's from 1915, entitled *Ma Mère Morte*, in which the dead woman lies in the background, her hands clasped around a rosary, mouth slackened by decay, while the foreground is given over to an eerie still-life, as a variety of medicine bottles with variously coloured labels catch and refract the light. I'd seen this painting, though not, as I recall, on that 1976 holiday, but I had thought it was housed elsewhere; yet here it almost is, in the Ensor room at Mu.ZEE, an image both deeply poignant and strangely matter-of-fact, one of a number of works (four drawings and two paintings, at least) that Ensor made in a furious bout of creativity during the three days after his mother died. She had supported him, financially and morally, through the hardest times and, if the gossip about her husband's drinking is to be trusted, she had borne her own portion of hardship. Now, in the painting, she is empty, undone, utterly cleansed by death. At the same time, she is not so much decaying as dissolving into the light, her body almost as transparent as the bottles in the foreground. This is not to suggest that Ensor, a confirmed atheist, wants us to see anything religious in these images (and the drawings he made at her deathbed, especially *Ma Mère Morte III*, are utterly uncompromising in this regard); what comes across instead is a sense of hard-won mortal release, both from hardship and from a lifetime of being masked.

Had she lived a few years more, my mother would have been partly gratified by the modest successes that came my way (a job in the civil service, then a middle-ranking position in the computer industry). But six months after that trip to Ostend, she was diagnosed with inoperable cancer; six months after that, we buried her in Corby cemetery, far from home, among people who were not her kin.

A fortnight before she died, I went into her room and found her lying very still, her eyes closed, the July sunlight spilling from the window onto her dressing table. She seemed impossibly remote, wonderfully other, the way those we love sometimes seem when dreaming – and I entertained the brief fantasy that, if I could talk to her as she lay in that suspended state, I could make her see that I'd never have been happy with what she thought of as happiness. That fantasy melted away, however, as I gazed at her face: serene, for the moment, unburdened, but just one more in a series of masks. Until then, I had assumed that all our masks were intended to conceal, and that what they concealed was the real self, a fixed entity who suffered pain and shame, a self that needed to be kept hidden, if only for its own protection or, in the case of my mother's dismay, to protect others. If I had paid more attention back in Ensor's house, however, I might have understood sooner that, of all our many life masks, none of them, not even the most fleeting or beatific, is any more true or false than any of the others.

Ensorhuis
Vlaanderenstraat 27, 8400 Oostende, Belgium
www.muzee.be/en/ensor

A Home from Home

MUSEUM OF FINE ARTS, BOSTON

Claire Messud

I first came to Boston as a teenager, enrolled in a boarding
school in the southern suburbs once attended by the young
T. S. Eliot. The school was founded in 1798 – which, in American terms, is old. For me, Boston was the stuff of novels: after a
childhood largely spent in Sydney and Toronto, in what seemed
to me a sort of Commonwealth periphery, I was headed, at last,
for a city about which memorable stories had been told and great
poems written.

It was also a city in which extraordinary paintings had been
collected. I loved the fact that so much of Boston's cultural identity had been confected by eccentric hybrids and expatriates,
by odd, thoughtful people who lived in between America and
Europe – Whistler (born in Lowell, Massachusetts, he was happy
when mistaken in Europe for a Russian), Sargent (born in Europe
to American parents, he consolidated his Boston connections
only later in life), Henry James (who, in spite of his British natu-
ralisation, is buried in the Cambridge Cemetery, half a mile from
my house), Edith Wharton ("I was a failure in Boston ... because
they thought I was too fashionable to be intelligent, and a failure
in New York because they were afraid I was too intelligent to be
fashionable"). With a French father, a Canadian mother and the
only American passport in the family, I was often anxious about
not being American enough: all these painters were reassuring

to me. Most of the United States has little interest in Europe, but that seemed not to be the case in Boston – not if you judged it by its art.

As a schoolgirl, I went rarely to the Museum of Fine Arts: the café was expensive, the gift shop didn't sell anything we wanted. We gravitated to the pavements of Harvard Square and Newbury Street, opting for the museum only in winter, to get out of the cold.

But somehow those adolescent visits impressed upon me a proprietorial sense about the place, an almost familial pride. When I returned 20 years later to live here with my husband and young children, I came back to the MFA as if to the embrace of extended family: there were my old friends, John Singleton Copley's *Watson and the Shark*, Thomas Sully's *The Torn Hat*, Sargent's *The Daughters of Edward Darley Boit*. They became my children's friends too. We joined the museum so as to visit for half an hour without guilt, and went briefly and often.

The children found their favourites, and have them still. My daughter Livia, at about six, tried to copy a Frank W. Benson painting of three kids in a boat. Her version hangs in her bedroom, and she thinks of the original as her own. My son Lucian likes Whistler's *Nocturne in Blue and Silver: The Lagoon, Venice*. We all like Childe Hassam's *Boston Common at Twilight*. With its grimed snow and sulphurous dusk, it evokes exactly our own winter evenings, erasing the 130 years between then and now.

The museum first opened its doors about a decade before that work was painted, on Independence Day 1876; it moved to its current quarters in 1909. There have been multiple expansions since, including the glassy new Art of the Americas wing, designed by Norman Foster, which opened in 2010. These big bright spaces sit surprisingly well around the original 1909

Beaux-Arts building, but the quiet core remains my favourite – sepulchral in the way of museums of my childhood, largely unwindowed, with broad corridors and staircases, hushed and echoey like a library, where every footfall speaks.

Rearranged in the new wing, some of our favourites are hard to find. *Watson and the Shark* used to be visible from miles away, illuminated at the end of a long corridor, but can now only be seen from much closer up, and seems a little cramped. More dismayingly, Sully's *The Torn Hat* – that boy who was like a cousin to Livia and Lucian – is no longer on display at all. After a brief and unfortunate spell behind glass in a mocked-up 19th-century sitting room, it has returned to the mysterious vaults where, I'm told, 95 per cent of the museum's holdings mutter in darkness. An early 19th-century American portrait of a long-nosed chap with what looked like a sock on his head has vanished too; though others, like Sargent's Boit sisters, have fared well and are now beautifully shown.

Still, it's a relief to return to our family's old haunts – to the damask-lined Koch Gallery with the European masters or to the newly reopened Impressionist gallery – and find things where we expect them to be. One unchanged corner which I always visit, hoping to find it empty, is the little vaulted room containing the 12th-century Spanish frescoes *Christ in Majesty with Symbols of the Four Evangelists*, taken from a small chapel in the Spanish Pyrenees. Mysterious and solemn but full of delight (who is that dancing chap in blue pleats, apparently raising a curtain, stage right?), these frescoes afford an opportunity for contemplation, a moment of retreat.

Even more than these figures with their beautiful Byzantine eyes, I come to this space to visit the Italian sculpture of the Virgin and Child, of the same vintage (above). Many renditions of the

Christ child make me smile (how oddly proportioned He can be, and what funny colours!), but this one brings me near to tears. He and his mother have strangely long heads, it's true, and in this way are stylised and foreign; but the folds of her dress, the precision of their limbs, the intensity of their embrace, the insistence of his small hand at the back of her neck, the yearning stretch of his face towards her cheek, his slight frown – I feel I know them, and their intense emotion. Theirs is at once the longing of every small child for its mother's body, and at the same time, strangely, discomfitingly, this Christ has about him something almost adult. The passion of their familial intimacy is recognisable across almost a millennium; this is the most human Christ I have ever seen.

In a completely different manner, Van Dyck's *Princess Mary* is totally present too. She's one of the few genuinely old paintings that my kids, it seems, can really see. The daughter of Charles I of England, Mary is captured around the time of her betrothal to William of Orange; and is fittingly satinned and bejewelled. Her sleeves look like they weigh a ton. But what's wonderful about young Mary – aside from the shimmer of her fabrics and the precision of their ornamentation, or the light folding of her childishly plump hands over her stomach – is the luminous rendition of her face and its familiar expression. My husband says, each time he sees her, "Oh, there's Amy!" because she so thoroughly resembles a former colleague of his.

Mary is wary – as she should be, standing stiffly for this great Flemish portraitist, about to be married off at the tender age of nine. She'd be widowed at 19, shortly after the execution of her father at the hands of Oliver Cromwell. And she'd be dead herself by 29. She looks as though she has some sense that her road will not be easy, and that all the luxurious garments in the world cannot protect her.

This Princess Mary came to America in the 1920s, sold by the Earl of Normanton and bought by Alvan Tufts Fuller, a wealthy car dealer who became governor of Massachusetts and lived to the ripe age of 80. If she could only have married him instead.

My kids love the Impressionist gallery best, as I did when I was young – the acid-bright Van Goghs, the hazy purple and blue Monets, the bright flower-filled Renoirs. Even now, as a teenager, my daughter has a frank affection for Degas's sculpture of the little 14-year-old dancer, her chin up and her hands behind her back, her tulle skirt rather grubby but her satin hair ribbon brand new. Livia will stand beside the glass case and mimic the girl's pose. She gave up ballet years ago, but she does it pretty well.

My own favourite Degas is the *Ballet Dancer with Arms Crossed*, an unfinished work bought at his posthumous studio sale in 1919. With her folded arms and averted gaze, she appears thoughtful, or near-tearful, possibly even sulky – it's hard to tell, just as it might be in life. Her face is largely in shadow, though her orangey lipstick glows; and her décolletage is an almost bruised grey, which, along with the black ribbon around her neck, imparts an atmosphere of darkness against the half-painted scarlet background. Her form is harshly outlined in black (how big and clumsy her right hand looks, when she is so generally graceful!); her skirt is pure white; and then, around her, the thin application of red paint allows the raw canvas to show through, balancing the white skirt with white patches on the left of the painting. Degas abandoned it in about 1872, but she remained for over 45 years in his studio: there's a strange intimacy in seeing this girl, whom the famously difficult painter could neither approve of nor relinquish, standing in her sad defiance on the wall.

Times have changed, and she no longer appears unfinished. A little blurred, off-colour, but intensely alive, she anticipates the contemporary work of, say, Marlene Dumas. Her presence, no less intense than Princess Mary's, is more emotional and interior, a presence that insists upon the filter of the artist's eye. As Edmond de Goncourt wrote after visiting Degas's studio, "Of all the men I have seen engaged in depicting modern life, he is the one who has most successfully rendered the inner nature of that life."

Which brings me back to Sargent. Everyone at our house has his or her particular favourite: mine is *The Daughters of Edward Darley Boit*. John Singer Sargent (1856–1925) was a portraitist of extraordinary facility. Claimed by Auguste Rodin as the "Van Dyck of our times", he had the gift, like Van Dyck with *Princess Mary*, of capturing surfaces so precisely that their interior is evoked. For many years a society painter, he was both adored and disdained for the elegance and sensuousness of his work.

There's a celebration of loveliness and ease that cumulatively can seem superficial, insufficient, a rich man's delight in velvet, brocade and Italian gardens, all of it underwritten by the wealthy and aristocratic patrons whose commissions for so many years occupied Sargent's time. But the jewel in the MFA's collection of his paintings is an antidote to this glossy illusory perfection, and proof that he was capable of darkness and complexity. *The Daughters of Edward Darley Boit* was painted in Paris in 1882, when the artist was in his mid-20s. The Boits were American friends of Sargent's, originally from Boston but living in luxury in the 8th arrondissement. The four girls – Mary Louisa, Florence, Jane and Julia – were painted in the foyer of their apartment, their white pinafores glistening in the gloom.

The MFA's Erica Hirshler tells us that Sargent was influenced by Velázquez's *Las Meninas*, which he'd studied at the Prado in Madrid. But the painting is far from traditional: only one of its subjects, four-year-old Julia, looks directly at the viewer, her legs stuck out before her and her doll upon her lap. For these girls, growing older appears to be a matter of retreat. Mary Louisa, the next in age, stands to the left of the painting, staring into the middle distance, her hands behind her back. Her frock is a warm old rose, the brushwork of her pinafore thick and brilliant, slashes of extra white upon her waistband: she is still very much in the light. But the two elder sisters, Florence and Jane, in black dresses beneath their pinafores, have stepped back into the corridor, and Florence has largely turned her back to us, leaning against one of the enormous Japanese vases that command as much attention as the girls. Florence's eye is on Jane, who has something lost about her, her stance and expression more tentative, more expectant, than her sisters'.

Only little Julia engages with the viewer, and only grown-up Florence engages with one of her sisters. The other two are abstracted, even isolated. As with Degas's dancer, their thoughts remain opaque, even as we can be certain that they're thinking.

Sargent, more than 20 years Degas's junior, was ultimately the less adventurous painter. In his later years, rather like Edith Wharton, he came to be seen as old hat, obsolete, the fusty representative of a lost world. But even today, there's something about this painting – the four sisters, none of whom would marry, and one of whom would struggle with mental illness – that is profoundly moving, and intimately familiar.

Those girls, like Princess Mary, enjoyed the blessings of privilege and wealth, which cushioned but could not save them. Thanks to their peripatetic parents, they lived between cultures and countries, just as they stand in the painting in their apartment's dark foyer on their way to somewhere else. There are advantages to this liminal state (I passionately believe in it, as someone also raised between different countries), but how relieving too, at the last, to have a home (not having had one, I wanted to make sure my children did); and how fitting a home the MFA is for these enigmatic Sargent girls, with one eye on the past and the other on the future.

Museum of Fine Arts, Boston
465 Huntington Avenue, Boston, MA 02115, United States
www.mfa.org

Where Sibelius Fell Silent

AINOLA, JÄRVENPÄÄ

Julian Barnes

There are two famous silences in the history of classical music: those of Rossini and Sibelius. Rossini's, which lasted nearly 40 years, was a worldly, cosmopolitan silence, much of it spent in Paris, during which time he co-invented tournedos Rossini. Sibelius's, which lasted nearly 30 years, was more austere, self-punishing and site-specific; and whereas Rossini finally yielded again to music, writing the late works he referred to as "the sins of my old age", Sibelius was implacable. He fell silent, and remained silent.

I first got to know his music almost half a century ago in recordings by Anthony Collins and the London Symphony Orchestra. The sleeves of those old Ace of Clubs LPs featured black-and-white photos of appropriately Nordic scenes: snowscapes, fjords, towering pine trees and so on. I think these images were mixed up with my early appreciation: there was a cool yet turbulent melancholy to them which I also found in the music, and which seemed to harmonise with my unrestful late-adolescent soul. But the music has stayed with me all my life, and, though generally uninterested in the lives of composers, I make an exception for Sibelius. I admire his mixture of puckish humour and obdurate high principle. During a conducting tour of England, he said in one post-concert speech, "I have plenty of friends here, and, naturally, I hope, enemies." He consoled a young colleague for a bad review with the words: "Always remember, there is no city in the world which has erected a statue to a critic." And during his final, silent years – he lived to the age of 91 – he noted at one point in his diary: "Cheer up! Death is round the corner." So for years I have wanted to visit Sibelius's house, 40 kilometres north of Helsinki, a region of lakes and pine forests and towering silver birches. For me it has always been a place with a dual, divided reputation: for both creation and destruction, for both music and silence.

Most artists' houses have had previous and subsequent owners. In some you feel only a vestige of the artist's presence; others have had their spirit crushed by museumification, by curatorial intervention and the accretion of study centres. The Sibelius house is one of those rare places where no other presence interferes with the genius loci: it is a house of, for, by, with and about Sibelius. He bought a one-acre plot at Järvenpää, near Lake Tuusula, in 1903. There was already an artists' colony here, but Sibelius was as much attracted by the empty landscape in which he loved to walk, by the swans and geese passing overhead.

In September 1904 he moved his family into the still unfinished house, which he named Ainola (the suffix "-la" meaning "place of") after his wife, Aino. Here they brought up their five daughters (a sixth died in infancy). Here Sibelius composed most of his major works, from the violin concerto of 1905 to the last five of his seven symphonies, and here he spent three decades not publishing a single note. When, in 1957, death's long round-the-corner wait ended, he was buried in the grounds; Aino lived on here for another 12 years; their joint tomb, a 6-foot square low bronze slab – which has the monumental inevitability of the later symphonies – was designed by their architect son-in-law Aulis Blomstedt. The five daughters, old themselves by the time of

Aino's death at the age of 97, sold the house and contents to the Finnish state in 1972, and it opened as a museum in 1974.

The house was designed (for no charge) by an architect friend, Lars Sonck, in the "National Romantic" style. It is essentially a grand log villa built on a heavy stone base and clad with weatherboard; in the grounds Aino designed a sauna house (with laundry room), laid out vegetable and flower gardens, and planted fruit trees, some of which still survive. Inside, the main rooms have heavy pine beams and those typically Scandinavian high stoves finished in glazed brick or tile. There is the feel of solid, continuous living to the place. Even the Sibeliuses' two housemaids were solid and continuous: both lasted nearly 60 years.

Almost nothing has changed (though Sibelius's original manuscripts have been removed to the national archives), and the place which once held Sibelius and his music still holds them both. The composer's white summer suit rests on a hanger in his study; his broad-brimmed Borsalino and stick are on a nearby table. Here is the Steinway grand he was given on his 50th birthday (though he composed in his head, not at the piano); there is a run of the National Geographic magazine covering the last five years of his life. On the Russian oak desk at which he worked from the time of his marriage in 1892 lies the wooden ruler Aino carved for him, with which he ruled his scores; also, an empty box of Corona cigars, and an elegant Tiffany photo frame, containing a portrait of Aino, through which the light streams. Open on the desk is a facsimile score of his greatest symphony, the Fourth. But the homely is never far away: in the kitchen, screwed to the wall, is an apple-coring machine which Sibelius brought back from one of his trips to America. Made of black cast iron, it is a Heath Robinson contraption of prongs, screws and blades which will peel, core and slice your apple at the turn of a handle. From the same trip he also brought his wife a Tiffany diamond; but it is the apple-corer that sticks in the mind.

Reminders of his fame are everywhere, from an enormous laurel wreath (now much dried) which once encircled him on a notable birthday to the multiple commemorative images made of him. Every time a plaster medallion of Finland's greatest artist was cast, he was given a personal copy, and most seem to have ended up on his walls. But genius had to co-exist with family life, and it was not always easy. "Our souls are worn down through continuous contact with one another," Sibelius wrote in his diary. And: "I am building a studio for myself – at least one. Next to me are all the children whose babbling and pranks ruin everything." But he never did build himself a studio; instead, he relocated his study upstairs and forbade the noise of any instrument while he was in the house. The children had to wait until he had gone for his daily walk to do their music practice.

The house, though comfortable and practical, is by no means extravagant. The visitor might reasonably conclude this was just a summer home, used by Sibelius to get away from the city. Not a bit of it. For most of his life he was in serious debt. At first these were a young man's debts, caused by his taste for high living: he was a committed drinker who would often go missing for days (but could always be located in "the best restaurant serving oysters and champagne"). And though the drinking was lifelong, and his tastes remained luxurious – that white suit came from Paris, his shoes and shirts were made for him in Berlin – this was not the reason why Aino kept chickens, laid out a vegetable garden, planted fruit trees and schooled her own children. Sibelius took on a huge debt when he built Ainola, and wasn't able to clear it for more than two decades. The website sibelius.fi contains a terrifying graph of his indebtedness for the period 1892–1926: it peaks at the equivalent of €300,000 today.

But, you will say, he was a world-famous composer. His music was constantly played; he was feted everywhere, not least in Britain – "the land without chauvinism", as he called it (we are to presume he was only talking musically). Constant Lambert, in his 1934 study *Music Ho!*, extravagantly called him "the most important writer [of symphonies] since Beethoven". Yale gave him a doctorate in 1914. How could such a man not afford to pay off the debts on his house? How come he was only saved from bankruptcy in 1910 by the intervention of generous patrons?

The answer lies mainly in history and the curious laws of copyright. When Sibelius started composing, Finland was part of the Russian empire, and Russia was not a signatory to international copyright treaties. So – apart from performing fees (and he often conducted) – Sibelius's income came from selling his work outright to music publishers. In 1905, for instance, he signed an agreement with Robert Lienau in Berlin to supply "four major works" in the coming year, the first of which went to pay for the sauna house Aino designed. Finland gained independence from Russia in 1919, but didn't sign the Berne Convention on Copyright until 1928 – by which time Sibelius had entered into his silence.

And in any case, you couldn't retrospectively claim copyright on what you had previously sold outright. To take the most egregious example: Sibelius composed his famous "Valse Triste" as part of the incidental music to *Kuolema* (1903). The following year he made two arrangements of the piece, each of which he sold outright for 100 marks (a little less than €3,000 in modern money). This may have seemed canny at the time. But "Valse Triste" was to become the best-known piece of music Sibelius ever composed; in the 1930s it was estimated to be the world's second most-played tune after "White Christmas" – yet from all the recordings and playings and sheet music Sibelius didn't receive a cent. He survived with the help of donations, national collections and a government pension; in 1912, he even thought of emigrating, whereupon the government raised his stipend and there were relieved newspaper headlines reading "Jean Sibelius remains in Finland". He finally became solvent at the age of 62, in 1927, and was eventually to die a fairly rich man. But it is an instructive story at a time when copyright is once again an issue, music piracy rife and "Don't-be-evil" Google has illegally digitalised hundreds of thousands of books still in copyright.

There is something heroic about those writers and artists who choose silence when it would be easier to supply profitable titbits to an adoring audience. Sibelius struggled with his Eighth Symphony for many years. He was constantly badgered about its progress; conductors and concert impresarios begged a foretaste. He always refused. Some believe that in the decades he worked on it he had finished only one movement. Sibelius himself claimed that he had "completed" the Eighth "many times" – though perhaps only in his head. In any event, at some point in the early 1940s, he piled the manuscript sketches of the Eighth plus a large quantity of other unfinished or (in his view) inadequate works into a big laundry basket, took them to the dining room, and, with Aino's help, began to feed them into the stove. After a while, Aino no longer had the strength to watch, and left the room, so she was unable to confirm exactly what had gone into the flames. But she reported that afterwards, "My husband became calmer and his attitude was more optimistic. It was a happy time."

The stove, made at the local brickworks, is chunky and rustic, with a glistening green finish (Sibelius saw colours as keys: green was F major, yellow D major). I bent down and tried to open the small steel doors, to see exactly where all that potential music had turned to ash. But they were screwed shut – not, it transpired, out of any piety, rather because in the years of Aino's widowhood the stove had been converted to electricity. Electricity also powered the library's shiny walnut-cased radiogram which the head of Philips gave Sibelius in the early 1950s. This was the last of a series of such instruments on which, all through the three decades of his personal silence, music had come into Ainola from Berlin, London, Paris and New York. Or from just 40 kilometres away. At the exact time Sibelius lay dying, on September 20th 1957, the Helsinki City Orchestra was playing his Fifth Symphony under Sir Malcolm Sargent. Naturally, the concert was being broadcast on Finnish radio, and Aino later recalled that she had been tempted to turn on the radiogram, in the hope that her husband's music might bring him back to consciousness; but in the end, she decided not to.

In his last year, Sibelius wrote in his diary: "The swans are always on my mind, and they lend magnificence to life. It is strange to note that nothing in the whole world, not in art, literature or music, has such an effect on me as these swans and cranes and bean geese. Their calls and their appearance."

If you stand in the grounds of Ainola today you are more likely to hear the steady thrum of traffic from a nearby road than the honk and wail of any passing wildlife. But the place retains its magic as a meeting-point of high art and practical living, of musical fame and apple-peeling machines, of conjured sounds and final silence.

Ainola
Ainolankatu, 04400 Järvenpää, Finland
www.ainola.fi

Wordsworth's Continuous Force

DOVE COTTAGE, GRASMERE

Ann Wroe

"**P**lease don't mention the rain," pleads the man in the Dove Cottage shop. It's hard not to; water is running down his anorak and dripping on the floor. Harsh drops beat against the windows, which show a misty procession of visitors shrouded in capes and hoods. "The Cumbrian Tourist Board will be very upset with me." In the porch of Dove Cottage, across the road, a basket which might have held broad beans or apples is now crammed with flimsy collapsible umbrellas in bright pink, blue and green.

It rains a lot in the Lake District, even in August, but tourists soon learn not to care. Water is intrinsic and essential to this place. I walked to Dove Cottage the hard way, through soaking bracken up to Alcock Tarn and down the other side. For the first half-mile I followed Greenhead Gill in spate, surging through high dark rocks hung with rain-dripping brambles, sycamore and ash. That furious brown water, swirling, foaming, leaping and thundering, represented for romantics the continuous force of thought: William Wordsworth's thought, as he walked here two centuries ago, humming and hawing along the roads as his neighbours observed him, making poems. That quiet pool, out of the flow, surrounded by mossy stones and where only one ripple enters, would have marked for him a point of equipoise and calm, in which words could be captured; that lace of foam, full of sparkling and bursting bubbles like a nebula of stars, suggested the transitoriness of human effort and human affairs. Wordsworth looked on these things, and mused as he looked. His presence has moulded the landscape as surely as streams and rain, so that the whole area round Grasmere, not just Dove Cottage, is a monument and museum to him.

Dove Cottage was the home to which, from 1799 to 1808, he returned from his walks, the nurturing cell in which many of his best poems were grown. His poetical career was long, lasting until 1850, and the muse gleamed only fitfully in the last decades. He had become a national poet, like Tennyson; the productivity was there, but not the light. By contrast, in Dove Cottage he wrote this:

> My heart leaps up when I behold
> A rainbow in the sky:
> So was it when my life began;
> So is it now I am a man;
> So be it when I shall grow old,
> Or let me die!

And these lines, almost too well known, on his sighting of wild daffodils in Ullswater:

> Continuous as the stars that shine
> And twinkle on the milky way
> They stretched in never-ending line
> Along the margin of a bay; ·
> Ten thousand saw I at a glance,
> Tossing their heads in sprightly dance.

And these, perhaps his greatest, from the "Immortality" ode:

> Our birth is but a sleep and a forgetting:
> The Soul that rises with us, our life's Star,

Hath had elsewhere its setting,
And cometh from afar;
Not in entire forgetfulness,
And not in utter nakedness,
But trailing clouds of glory do we come
From God, who is our home.

The blaze of inspiration in these poems – the sense of each object "apparell'd in celestial light" – is all the more striking because Dove Cottage is a dark, poky place. The steep slopes of Rydal Fell and Nab Scar crowd in this tiny, limewashed house to north, south and east; only to the south-west does the view open up to Grasmere Lake and the facing mountains, chased by shifting colours and shadows of the clouds, as Dorothy, Wordsworth's sister, often described them.

The cottage was once a pub, the Dove and Olive Bough, on the road to Rydal; the word "snug" might have been coined for it. As Wordsworth entered, shrugging off his wet coat in the vestibule, he would have found a welcoming fire in a small, low room wainscotted in dark oak from floor to ceiling. The panelling hid walls deep-stained with drinkers' tobacco smoke. The latticed window, one-third larger now than it was then, would have looked out mostly on the glistening slabs of slate used (illegally) by William and Dorothy to enclose a patch of garden in front of the house. A dry stone wall has long replaced them, now overgrown with ivy, herb robert and wild strawberries. It may not be authentic, but it seems right. In the rain, each thin stalk and green leaf is diamonded with drops.

To me the meanest flower that blows can give
Thoughts that do often lie too deep for tears.

The entrance room, called the "Houseplace", contains a primitive painting of a mournful, cross-eyed dog. This is Pepper, a gift to the Wordsworths from Sir Walter Scott, and a reminder that there were children here, at least for a few years. In 1802 William married Mary Hutchinson; by the time they moved out there were three toddlers, who sometimes slept in a recess under the kitchen table, tucked in baskets, and sometimes in a minuscule unheated room upstairs, insulated by Dorothy with pages from the *Times*. (The pages have had to be replaced, which the Wordsworth Trust has done with great care and ingenuity, finding pages of just the right date, including one from 1800 with an advertisement for the second edition of Wordsworth's and Coleridge's revolutionary democratisation of poetry, the *Lyrical Ballads*.) The newspaper room, as it is called, sums up much of the character of this place. From remote Grasmere the Wordsworths kept up keenly with the news of the day, both through papers and a stream of visitors, but the real use of good rag newspaper was to keep infants warm. This was a house where nothing was wasted: where dogwood twigs from the garden, stripped and frayed, made toothbrushes, and where used tea-leaves were dried and sent to friends.

The kitchen tells the same tale. Two objects, on the mantelpiece over the (later) range, evoke the importance of frugality – and of light. One is a candle-mould, into which melted mutton fat and beeswax were poured and cooled. The other is a rushlight holder, in which the rush may be adjusted diagonally for one person reading or writing, or horizontally, burning at both ends, for two. There were usually two people working here in the evenings: William dictating, from his favourite "cutlass" chair or cane-seated couch (both still here), and Dorothy or Mary transcribing. The mere light of rush or candle did not go very far; it illuminated, perhaps, the table top. When several were reading and sewing, their heads were bent companionably together. From out on the benighted fells, the window would have shone like a star.

The Wordsworth household at Grasmere was a triangle of poet, sister and wife. Both women waited on the great man, cooking his mutton chops and mending his thick grey socks, watching anxiously how he ate and how he slept, for poetry-making wore out his nerves. Both loved him, and he loved them. His relationship with Dorothy and hers with him seem to have been perfectly correct, sealed by brotherly-sisterly tenderness and mutual inspiration. Nonetheless there is often a frisson in this house, of feelings suppressed. It touches you especially in William's bedroom, which became Dorothy's in 1802, and from which she watched swallows building and rebuilding in the eaves over the window. It now contains William's and Mary's nuptial bed, very small and cosy under a patterned quilt; Dorothy nailed up the valances and hessian hangings on this bed to make it even cosier, a love nest. The mirror on the washstand, which was Dorothy's, now reflects the bed in its dim, spotted glass. On it lies William's tiny suitcase, which she probably packed for him: for four weeks in France in 1802, when he was revisiting his first French lover, one day-shirt, one night-shirt, a notebook and a pen.

Not many objects are kept in the cottage now. They have gone to the Wordsworth Museum up the road, or to the splendid modern library and archive at the Jerwood Centre next door to it. But in glass-fronted cupboards upstairs lie Wordsworth's wooden skates, which he nailed onto his shoes ("All shod with steel/We hissed along the polished ice in games/ ... and every icy crag/Tinkled like iron"). There are delicate teacups, whose worn rims still seem to hold the murmur of conversation, and lurking nearby a small, dark phial of Kendal Black Drop laudanum, the cure for most aches and pains in this house. But perhaps most moving is a small piece of bright blue stone that was found, after his death, in Wordsworth's dressing-case. "Mr W's eyes have been cured by one of our visitors, Mr Reynolds, who prescribed touching them with the Blue Stone which acted like magic on them", wrote Sara Hutchinson, Mary's sister, in 1826. A pair of spectacles on the same shelf, with small dark lenses, confirm that those eyes, which saw "into the life of things", were physically weak, and often hurt him.

On all the back windows of the cottage the garden presses in, lushly green and shining with rain. Roses, heavy with their soaking, lean against the glass, and sprays of fern fall down like water. The lawn is slippery and steep, rising to the woods and the fell. William and Dorothy laboured on this "little Nook of mountain ground", and Dorothy recorded it all in her journal: stringing up the scarlet beans, cutting the pea sticks, transplanting "raddishes", and William's digging of the shallow, muddy well. They grew most of the vegetables they ate with their almost sempiternal porridge. But this was also a place where Nature and her moving, affecting power might be brought in from outside, corralled with the ferns and columbines and marsh-marigolds which the Wordsworths had purloined from the lakeside. In this "Dear Spot" William built a terrace, where he could pace back and forth as he did along the roads, gazing over the lake and the favourite mountains, Helm Crag and Silver How, to find inspiration. "We walked backwards & forwards", wrote Dorothy on March 17th 1802, until "William kindled, and began to write the poem." Another time, at the end of April, "Walked backwards &

forwards with William – he repeated his poem to me – then he got to work again & would not give over" (a lovely northern note) " – he had not finished his dinner till 5 o clock." Thanks to Dorothy, we know he was writing his lines "To the Small Celandine".

> Ere a leaf is on a bush,
> In the time before the thrush
> Has a thought about her nest,
> Thou wilt come with half a call,
> Spreading out thy glossy breast
> Like a careless Prodigal;
> Telling tales about the sun
> When we've little warmth, or none.

An "Indian shed", now speculatively reconstructed, was built at the top of the garden, and beneath it a "sodded wall" from which they watched tourists in landaus going past. One wonders what the tourists made of them: the lanky, aquiline poet and the thin, dreamy women, their hands still red from chores, lying on their cloaks on the orchard grass to look at blossom falling and listen to the birds.

In mid-afternoon sunlight falls on Dove Cottage, unexpectedly, like a grace. The Japanese tourists are astonished. They come out of the back door blinking, not needing their umbrellas. As Wordsworth did, they watch "the dancing of shadows amid a press of sunshine", washed by the last gleams of the rain. It is easy to lose confidence in Lake District weather. But in the end – as in the dingiest corners of this unassuming house – the light that he evoked with such power is always palpably there.

> The stars pre-eminent in magnitude,
> And they that from the zenith dart their beams

(Visible though they be to half the earth,
Though half a sphere be conscious of their brightness)
Are yet of no diviner origin,
No purer essence, than the one that burns,
Like an untended watch-fire, on the ridge
Of some dark mountain; or than those which seem
Humbly to hang, like twinkling winter lamps,
Among the branches of the leafless trees;
All are the undying offspring of one
Sire: Then, to the measure of the light vouchsafed,
Shine, Poet! in thy place, and be content.

Dove Cottage
Grasmere, Cumbria LA22 9SH, UK
www.wordsworth.org.uk/visit/dove-cottage.html

Agony to Ecstasy

THE PRADO, MADRID

John Lanchester

My engagement with museums has been a game of three parts – so far – and in all three of them the question of children has been defining. In the first third, I was a child; in the second, I wasn't; in the third, I'm a parent. My sense of what museums are, and are for, has changed accordingly.

Museums are places of education, and childhood is where most of our education takes place, so it's only natural that museums should have a relationship with children. That's the theory, anyway. In practice, during my childhood, museums were places of torture. It went both ways: my parents tortured me by taking me to them, and I tortured them back by being irrevocably, inconsolably bored. This usually happened on trips abroad, because Hong Kong, where we lived, was short on museums – one of the great things about it, I then thought. When we went on holidays, they would drag me, at times literally, around great museums of the world. The Topkapi Palace in Istanbul was one; the National Palace Museum in Taipei, home of the treasures taken into Taiwanese exile by the Kuomintang, was another. I now think these were extraordinary places to have visited, and I salute my parents for their imagination in doing so. At the time, though, for a pre-adolescent boy interested in science fiction, football and chess, these were lower circles of hell.

The switch wasn't thrown until my gap year. I spent a few

months Interrailing and hitch-hiking around Europe, and in the course of that trip, at 19 years old, I caught the bug. Or, maybe, I'd been carrying the infection without realising it. Going to look at pictures was partly a practical matter. It gave you something to do. When you arrived in a new city, the first thing you did was find the youth hostel, and the second was go to the main museum. That museum gave a focus and a point to being in a strange city. I saw a huge Picasso retrospective in Copenhagen; I saw Munch's *The Scream* in Oslo, the painting hitting me with all the more force because I came on it unexpectedly, without build-up; I saw Eila Hiltunen's Sibelius monument in Helsinki; I toured the National Archaeological Museum in Athens; I saw Dürer's self-portrait in the Alte Pinakothek in Munich.

That afternoon in Munich was full of wonders. I came out of the museum, found a beer garden and in it saw something more extraordinary and mysterious than the art works I'd just been studying: a group of four kids my own age, sitting at a trestle table in front of litres of beer. Then the astonishing thing happened: they looked at their watches, looked at each other, nodded, and got up and left, *without finishing their drinks*. Each of them left undrunk about a third of a litre of lager. I had never seen such a thing, had no idea it was possible. None of my friends, nobody I knew, had ever not finished a drink. It was clear that the world was a bigger and stranger place than I had guessed.

The climax of that trip, from the museum-going point of view, was the Prado. It was the last leg of my three-month Interrail ticket; after that it would be a straight shot, Madrid to Calais, then the ferry home. The Prado was also, as it is still, the only museum that is a great city's uncontested number-one attraction. The Louvre is high on lists of reasons to visit Paris, as the British Museum is for London and the Met for New York, but the

only museum which has unique status as the city's single greatest glory is the Prado. I had changed so much over those months
that by then I was really looking forward to it: a trip to a city, just
to visit a museum. My younger self (not to mention my parents)
would have been incredulous.

The two things I remember with most force from that first
visit to the Prado were, first, a strong feeling of the cultural dis-
tinctiveness of Spain, and, second, a powerful sense that the heart
of the collection was about madness, delirium, sex and death. I
was 19, so I thought: great! Anyone with even the faintest interest in art has seen reproductions of Hieronymus Bosch's great
masterpieces *The Haywain* and *The Garden of Earthly Delights*. I had
looked at a guidebook, so had to that extent encountered the pictures already. The reality of them, however, was startlingly more
forceful than I'd expected.

As a teenager, whatever the intensity of your preoccupa-
tions, you usually know that you are also trying on ideas and
attitudes; sketching versions of the self you might settle down to
be. Your engagement with the world outside your head is also an
attempt at getting to know yourself, and so it can be both deep
and superficial at the same time: you can wear heavy things
lightly, often too lightly. I had a great interest in sex, madness,
darkness, magic, death, but at the same time on some level knew
that I was playing with ideas. Bosch, though: he wasn't playing.
Those inexplicable, flat, horrible pictures – bizarre even in their
colour palette, in the crazed pinkness of the Garden – were not a
game. That picture is also, in a way every 19-year-old can immediately understand, boiling with sex, though it is also insistently,
hysterically sexless, because there is no actual sex in it. These
naked bodies are in every kind of extremis except that. The
painting is a depiction of excess, abandonment and delirium,

and at the same time has an overpowering sense of operating under taboo.

In the same room at the Prado, then and now, is Bruegel's *Triumph of Death*. This was another picture which even if you didn't have a clue about painting – i.e., were me – you could immediately tell was a masterpiece. Now, revisiting the Prado 30-plus years later, I see that picture as both a record of one kind of war, medieval and religious, and the precursor of another, the modern conflict in which death is a juggernaut, an indiscriminate harvester of mainly civilian lives. It seems to me today a depiction of something that has happened and keeps on happening. On that first visit, though, I thought it was another fantasy, another vision; an appropriate picture for a despotic monarch, Felipe II, to hang in his palace. It was also Felipe who acquired the Bosch paintings and built the black, sinister Escorial palace just outside the city. The mad king in his mad castle with his mad paintings, and in another room a painting of his mad wife, Mary Queen of Scots, her tight, disapproving face radiating fanaticism: the museum felt like a vortex of culture and madness and national identity.

The artist I'd been looking forward to encountering was Goya, whom I "knew" about because he was a favourite of Hemingway's, who was a favourite of mine. I didn't find what I was looking for. I think that was partly because I made a mistake which it's easy to make: the Prado layout has the "black paintings", the psychic nadir and artistic high point of Goya's last years, on the lower floor, where, if you're going round the Spanish rooms in sequence (which you must), you will encounter them before you've come across the paintings of his early career and middle life. That's wrong: you need to see them in chronological sequence to get the full impact. On this second visit, I made sure to do it the right way around.

At 19, I hit the black paintings first and couldn't really see what the fuss was about. After Bosch and Bruegel the horror seemed low-key, merely personal. *The Third of May 1808*, a masterpiece which both depicts and foresees so much, also left me a little flat. I'd read lots of books about Vietnam. I knew about wartime atrocities, thanks, man.

James Fenton observes somewhere that you don't judge great art, it judges you. I failed the Goya test. Going back to the Prado a third of a century later, Goya hasn't changed or grown up, because he didn't need to, but I have, and the power and poignancy of his life in painting seem to me unmatched. The thing that unlocked his work for me was a remark made by a friend, that Goya was "the Mozart who passed into darkness". Yes: Goya's earlier work has the sublime grace and power and ease and imaginative fertility of Mozart. Nobody's formal portraiture is more expressive than Goya's, achieving as it does the quadruple trick of formal beauty, external realism, psychological realism and also telling you what the painter felt about the subject. To compare his portrait of Charles IV with his of Ferdinand VII is to know what it felt to be liked or loathed by Goya, and also what each of these men was like. The clothed and naked Maya are a famous set-piece, but his tiny picture of the Duchess of Alba rowing with her Duenna is even more sensually charged, funny and cheeky, her body unmistakably sexy and energetic under her black gown.

The black paintings, when you come on them in the right order, are about a retreat from public life, from pleasure and sex and company and the world. Their titles, even the fact of their having titles, is misleading. They were paintings Goya made for his own … his own … the right word is elusive: pleasure? use? distraction? self-torment? He had moved just outside Madrid and lived in a house known as the Quinta del Sordo, the House of the Deaf Man. The paintings, made straight onto the walls, had no titles, and that adds to their sense of unease, of having emerged from formlessness and nightmare: faces screaming in fear or anger or reproach (very much a deaf man's image of horror); a monster feeding on a child, presumably his own; a crowd of brute faces worshipping a goat; hovering witches. To have been as much a creature of the world as Goya, and to have loved the things of the world as much as he did, and to have come to this place, deaf and bitter and betrayed and lonely, and yet still capable of creating art of this intimacy and potency. Only Picasso has as much sense of having painted a whole span of life as Goya: a life in full.

Why on earth would I have been able to understand that at 19? I sometimes joke that art should be strictly 18-rated. At least it would give children a sense that it's dangerous, that real things are at stake. Also, I'd have been spared many hours of childhood boredom. As a parent, I think that museums are largely wasted on children, that parents risk giving their children a homeopathic dose of culture and the past, just enough to cure them of an interest for the rest of life. At the Prado this year, there were groups of primary schoolchildren sitting on the floor, on the receiving end of lectures about the *Garden of Earthly Delights* and the *Third of May*, paintings of, it seems to me, entirely adult horror. That looks like a mistake, a waste, a misunderstanding of what art is. I wouldn't do that to my own children. To be fair, they wouldn't let me. At the same time, I find myself wondering whether, if I hadn't been dragged around in my childhood, I would now be voluntarily self-dragging. Maybe the conversation of art is, like most conversations, one where you have to listen for a while before you can join in for yourself. I suppose what I'm saying is, perhaps my parents were right.

The Prado
Paseo del Prado, Calle Ruiz de Alarcón 23, 28014 Madrid, Spain
https://www.museodelprado.es/en

The Museum of Heartbreak

THE MUSEUM OF BROKEN RELATIONSHIPS, ZAGREB

Aminatta Forna

As I enter the room, a kissing couple draw quickly apart. He crosses to study something on the other side of the small room; she studies the description on the display in front of her. He's wearing a hooded sweatshirt; she has a red bag slung around her. As they're very young, it seems unlikely that they are having an illicit affair, so perhaps I have just embarrassed them.

After they are gone, I look at the exhibit they were standing in front of. It's a broad-bean heater. "There's a saying in Egypt that broad beans are best served warmed up", reads the tag. "Our relationship never got warmed up, but the friendship remained as strong as dried broad beans." The relationship, the tag explains, lasted from 1990 to 1991, so it coincided with the war of independence here in Croatia. I wonder whether the two things are connected – whether the war was the reason that this love foundered, or went unspoken, or missed its mark.

Against the opposite wall is a shaving kit given by a 17-year-old girl to her married lover in the late 1980s. When he donated it to this museum, the married man wrote: "I hope she doesn't love me any more. I hope she doesn't know she was the only person I ever loved."

Almost everything in the museum – room after white-painted room of illuminated display tables, stuffed animals, china dogs, silk dresses, coats and hats and books, ornaments of plastic

171

or glass or ceramics, photograph albums, timepieces and domestic appliances – repeats the same message: that love ends in loss. Love ends in loss, always. Only the broad-bean heater, still in its original box, suggests that a love unrealised may yet yield some measure of happiness.

I first came across the Museum of Broken Relationships while walking through Gradec in the old town of Zagreb early last summer. I had come to trace the footsteps of characters in my new novel, *The Hired Man*, who move to this city and one day have lunch in the Hotel Dubrovnik. I had first imagined the scene, relying on written accounts of the hotel and of Tomislav Square, where they watch the 100-year-old trees being felled. Later, I'd come to Zagreb with my husband to walk the scene through, to make sure of my facts. The square and the hotel were close together, closer than I'd imagined, but the drive from Zadar to Zagreb took hours and by the time we arrived we were too late for lunch at the hotel. Instead, we wandered into the old town where, on a side street below St Mark's Square, we happened upon the museum.

On the right, as you enter, is a small café, on the left a gift shop and the ticket desk. Ahead of you lies a series of rooms, each bearing a name. Some are as fanciful as the names of racing thoroughbreds – Allure of Distance, Whims of Desire. From Rage and Fury you can turn right and pass through Tides of Time and into Rites of Passage, which in turn leads to Paradox of Home (wherein I found the guilty couple). If instead you walk straight through Rage and Fury you will come to Resonance of Grief, and the final room, Sealed by History. This part of the old town is mainly composed of municipal buildings, and the museum's stone-floored rooms may formerly have served as offices. Resonance of Grief, whose walls bear old white tiles, looks as if it might once have been a urinal.

Next to each exhibit is a tag indicating where and when the relationship took place, and offering the donor's explanation of the gift. So, in the first room, on the wall above a pair of black leather boots: "Biker boots. 1996–2003. Zagreb, Croatia. I bought this pair of boots for Ana before our trip to Paris. Later on, other girls wore them too, but they always remained Ana's boots."

Olinka Vistica and Drazen Grubisic, the museum's founders, were once a couple in love. One hot summer some years ago they stopped being in love and began to divide the contents of their apartment. Theirs had been an amicable split, though no less sad for that, and so they sorted through the rooms together, parsing shared memories of their relationship. Cups, CDs, ashtrays, coffee grinders, pans, rugs, books, badges, scarves: "even the most banal object [had] a story to tell." These were the sorts of objects every well-meaning friend, every self-help manual, every magazine article offering advice on how to recover from heartbreak urged people like them to throw away, burn, break or give to charity – to get rid of at all costs. When love ends there must be no reminders. But this pair didn't wish to do any such thing. They wondered at the mercilessness of disposing of the evidence of love that may have given years of joy and much pleasure. They decided to curate a travelling exhibition of donated items, to offer bereft lovers the chance to create a ritual, an alternative to the vandalism proposed by the self-help manuals – "a chance to overcome an emotional collapse through creation", as the printed sign above Ana's boots tells newcomers. Since then, the first collection of objects has multiplied many times, finding a permanent home in Zagreb. A travelling exhibition has toured the world, collecting objects as it goes, offering the broken-hearted, betrayed and bereaved of Buenos Aires and Berlin, of Cape Town, Istanbul, Houston and even of Sleaford in Lincolnshire a chance to share the stories of their items.

It seemed to me, on my first visit, that Olinka and Drazen had hit on something – for what is there to do with all those objects one can no longer bear to look upon? Our homes are filled with fetishes: heirlooms, gifts, things we bring back from distant lands, all imbued with emotion. There on my bookshelf is the blue tin teapot from Timbuktu, on the mantelpiece a carved stone given to me by a beloved godchild, in the kitchen the collars of dead dogs hanging from a peg. All these accumulated totems, heaved over the course of a lifetime from home to home, are the physical evidence of having lived: our memories made solid.

When I met my husband he gave me a die-cast medal showing the Tibetan animal horoscopes, which he'd bought on his travels. I put the medal on a key-ring and carried it around the world; I had it with me when I bought the teapot in Mali. In return I gave him a talisman of my own, a small brass figure from Sierra Leone which, to this day, he too keeps on a key-ring. In *The Hired Man* a young boy, Duro, is given a small ceramic heart by his first love. It remains in his pocket during the years of his military service and even when she is married to someone else. Exchanging tokens of our love is something we all do.

It was winter when I returned to Zagreb. Empty lots housed great mounds of snow shifted from the streets. Gone were the outdoor cafés and street vendors. I found myself booked, by coincidence, into the Hotel Dubrovnik, where the older citizens of Zagreb, wearing hats and coats with fur collars, were taking their morning coffee in the café exactly as they must have been doing since the hotel was built in 1929.

After breakfast I set off for the museum with a map, uncertain I could remember the way. The map took me a different route, past the cathedral, into which I wandered briefly to view the statues of the saints, and through the Stone Gate, beneath whose arches lies a shrine to the Madonna. In one corner, a woman was selling candles, while another woman prayed in front of a painting contained behind ornate iron railings. In 1731 a great fire destroyed the old wooden gate and everything that surrounded it, except, so the legend goes, the painting of the Madonna and Child, which is therefore believed to possess magical powers.

How like worshippers are the visitors to the museum, standing with heads bowed and hands clasped, moving slowly and silently from one relic to the next. It's a weekday morning, and the place is relatively empty. There are just a handful of young couples, and a few middle-aged women wearing the kind of chic travel clothing favoured by the French and Italians. Seven out of ten of the museum's visitors are women, I'm told, and most are under 40.

In the first room, alongside Ana's boots, are items that carry the memory of love which has passed and for which there is no place in the landscape of a new love. The mood is of longing. The objects in the next room carry memories of pain – greater, it would seem, than the love that preceded it. Behind a crystal curtain in Whims of Desire a pair of fake breasts juts from the wall, donated by a woman whose husband obliged her to wear them during love-making, until she left him. An axe has been sent from Berlin by a woman whose lesbian lover left her for another. While the two were on holiday together, the abandoned lover bought this axe. "In the 14 days of her holiday, every day I axed one piece of her furniture." She arranged the pieces neatly, waited until her former lover came back to collect her belongings, then showed them to her.

I move on swiftly towards the back room, where I am drawn by a red light that flashes from one of the display tables. In front of it is the young couple I'd caught kissing earlier. They are standing with their arms around each other's waist, and she has her head on his shoulder. When they move on a few moments later, I take my turn to look at the flashing object.

Here is a story to make you cry. After 13 years, when their love has mellowed into friendship, a husband leaves his wife. She takes their little dog with her, because the husband feels she needs the comfort more than he. For months he suffers from depression, perhaps he misses her, we are not told. Whatever he feels, he does not return to the marriage. She worries for him. One day he receives a package from her containing a few small things, each of which, he says, "broke my heart a little more and were mostly about her wanting to take care of me, even though she was the one suffering". Among them was a dog collar with a red flashing light, which she had bought for the dog so that he should never get lost. In the year since they parted the husband had spoken to her of feeling "lost". After they have been apart for a year, his wife checks into a hotel in a strange town. There she takes her own life. The flashing light, he says, reminds him of her heartbeat.

As I walk round the museum, it's stories like this – shocking, arresting, upsetting – that absorb my attention. Reflecting on the place later, I find my thoughts returning to less dramatic exhibits: Ana's boots, or the wedding album donated by a woman who was miserable in her first marriage, but is now happy in her second. Thinking about these, I feel cautiously uplifted. They seem to show that, however long it takes and however painful the process, people can learn about themselves, and about love.

I cross Jelačić Square, which used to be called Republic Square, and I think how in most ways this country, after years of communism and then the war, feels unchanged from when I first came here, in 1969. I remember the holiday vividly though I was only five years old – standing on a beach with my sister, while my mother and her new husband called to me from a wooden boat offshore to swim to them. I was frightened: I wanted my rubber ring, but it was on the boat and between us lay 50 metres of water. The boatman's nephew, who must have been eight or nine years old, picked up my rubber ring, dived into the water and brought it to me. For the rest of the holiday, he was my hero. I remember, because it was the very first time I ever felt that way about a boy.

How much there remained to know.

The Museum of Broken Relationships
Ćirilometodska 2, 10 000 Zagreb, Croatia
https://brokenships.com

The Quiet Theatres

THE SIR JOHN RITBLAT TREASURES GALLERY, LONDON

Andrew Motion

Thanks to the rise of the literary festival, writers are now forced to get out and about, meeting readers, making new ones, fielding questions. There are two kinds of question you can rely on: about ideas – where do they come from? and about method. Do you use a pen or pencil, do you write early or late in the day, do you change much as you go along or depend on revisions? It's easy to sound blasé about this. When Philip Larkin was interviewed for the *Paris Review*, he was asked how he came up with the image of a toad to represent work, and he replied: "Sheer genius!" But the fact is that both readers and writers are intrigued by the most primitive details of how things get written. Readers because the mystery of being a writer is deepened by its close proximity to ordinary practice (writing everyday letters, writing memos at work or, now, writing e-mails), and writers because they want to establish a dependable procedure that will produce the goods on a regular basis.

Manuscripts are the quiet theatres in which these dramas are performed and preserved. My own fascination with them began when I began writing myself, as a teenager, about 40 years ago. My mentor was Geoffrey Keynes, the surgeon and brother of Maynard, whose extraordinary library at his house near Cambridge included manuscripts that he would hand me with an impressive mixture of reverence and familiarity. I remember in particular the manuscript of Virginia Woolf's essay "On Being Ill", which her husband, Leonard, had given Geoffrey as a thank-you for helping her survive one of her bouts of self-destructive depression. The fluent script, the purple ink, the flying revisions: all these were fascinating. But what struck me more powerfully than anything was the simple fact of the thing. It was irrefutable proof that something astonishing in its intelligence and association had been produced by a human being who sat down one day, unscrewed her pen-top and simply went to work.

This was my first important lesson in the power of manuscripts – and in how their value depends on a mixture of things, what Larkin once called "the meaningful" and "the magical". By meaningful, he meant the way manuscripts tell us about dating and timing and speed of production, and about the power of second thoughts (or tenth ones). All the things, in fact, that are indispensable to scholars, and compelling for fans. By magical, he meant the gut amazement of thinking, wow, Keats (or Tennyson, or Wilde, or Hardy) had this piece of paper when it was a blank sheet, their hand touched it, their breath swarmed all over it, and they made something immortal out of nothing.

My second lesson was more remote, yet even more decisive. As I began to write poems in my teens, I also began buying them. One of the first books I owned was the *Collected Poems of Wilfred Owen*, edited by Cecil Day Lewis, with a memoir of Owen by Edmund Blunden. I got it because we'd been doing Owen in English, and for the first time poetry had grabbed me. (My family were country people, not in the least bookish. My mum read a bit of Iris Murdoch, that sort of thing; my dad claimed to have read half a book in his life – *The Lonely Skier*, by Hammond Innes.)

In an appendix to Owen's poems was a reproduction of a part of the manuscript of his great sonnet "Anthem for Doomed

Youth", showing not only the corrections that Owen himself had made to his first draft, but also those added by his friend Siegfried Sassoon. (Owen had shown him the poem at Craiglockhart Hospital in Edinburgh in 1917, when they were both recovering from shellshock.) The lesson for a tyro poet was unmistakable: take advice from people who know more than you do; don't trust the authority of first thoughts; mix inspiration with perspiration.

When I left school and went to read English at Oxford, the effect of these early encounters was continually reinforced, as the Bodleian Library put on regular shows of manuscripts in its collection. There was a draft of Shelley's "Ode to the West Wind", in which his spidery brownish script hurtled across the page as though the wind itself were sweeping it onwards – before ending with a date, October 25th, that rooted it in a particular moment.

Later, when I stayed in Oxford to write a thesis on the poet Edward Thomas, killed at Arras in 1917, manuscripts became a part of my daily life. Later still, when I was appointed Poet Laureate in 1999, I made it my business to campaign on behalf of British libraries, and authors, in the hope that the flow of manuscripts from British hands into American holdings might be partly redirected towards British libraries. Nothing against America or its libraries: I just think there's a value – academic, philosophical, emotional – in keeping things close to their point of origin.

The British Library has played a significant part in this campaign, which is appropriate, given that it hosts Britain's most remarkable permanent display of manuscripts. This is thanks partly to the fact that it has an enormously rich collection (to which it continues to make bold additions – most recently the J. G. Ballard archive) and partly to John Ritblat, the property magnate, whose generosity enabled the gallery that bears his name to be built within the library when it moved to its present site in St Pancras in 1998.

The gallery is easy to take for granted. Compared with the visual arts, the thrill and beauty of manuscripts are not widely celebrated, but this single mid-sized room, with its black walls, lowered lights and atmosphere of something approaching reverence, is one of the world's great treasure troves. It is a place of delight as well as learning, and of astonishment as well as understanding. Whenever I have a group of students, I insist that they come here: it's an Eng. Lit. version of the geography field trip.

Some parts of the collection are on permanent display – the material relating to Lewis Carroll and the "Alice" books, and the manuscripts of several songs by The Beatles. These songs are as good a place to start as any, as they abolish any idea that displays of this sort are somehow dusty, or of narrow academic interest. The Beatles' music and words continue to live in the world as few other kinds of writing have ever managed to do. Yet their composition, judging by the evidence here, depended on a similar blend of luck and labour. Paul McCartney's "Michelle" turns out to be based on a tune he first tried to get down when he was at school, "in an attempt", the label says, "to write a French-sounding song at the time when the bohemian Parisian Left Bank was a fashionable influence on art students". Several years later John Lennon suggested that if Paul wanted it to sound French, he'd better use some French words – hence "ma belle" and so on. It was hardly Proust, but it did the trick, and the song was included on *Rubber Soul*. It became the only Beatles track ever to be named Song of the Year at the Grammys.

The value common to all eight Beatles documents on display here is their magical ordinariness – the way their instant recognisability and lasting fame sprang from the most modest origins.

"A Hard Day's Night" was written very fast, in biro and felt-tip, in response to a phrase Ringo Starr had used to describe the Beatles' hectic life, on a birthday card that was intended for the infant Julian Lennon. "I Want to Hold Your Hand" has a similar air of speed – and at the end of it John Lennon has written, as if commenting on himself as a teacher: "3/10 See me". The same sort of sublime ordinariness confronts us in the manuscript of "Yesterday". This may be the most covered pop song in history, with over 3,000 versions recorded, but it started life as something very simple: everyday words on an everyday page.

The Beatles' manuscripts are marvellous things – so fresh in their appeal, and so vulnerable in their lack of self-importance. And when we turn away from them, we find ourselves among texts that lie at the other end of the spectrum. These include what are probably the greatest treasures in the gallery: a fragment of the Psalms, dating from the third century AD and written on papyrus; the Codex Sinaiticus, which is the earliest complete New Testament to have been written in Greek; and the Codex Alexandrinus, dating from the first half of the fifth century, which is one of the most important manuscripts of the whole Bible to survive in Greek.

Here the notion of manuscript-as-revelation finds its highest as well as its most literal expression – as it also does in the immensely beautiful ancient and sacred texts relating to Jainism, Hinduism, Islam and Judaism. And in the Garland Sutra from Korea, one of the most important Mahayana Buddhist scriptures, which was created on mulberry paper between 1390 and 1400 and is exquisitely illuminated with images of deer, rabbits, bears, birds and shaggy-furred human beings. In a sense that is strictly speaking unique, these objects are at once distillations (small enough to be contained in a single look, and to be absorbed by a single mind) and limitless eruptions of idea and feeling. To look at them is to contemplate nothing less than a large part of the history of the world. No picture, no piece of music, however lovely and celebrated, has had this effect on the same scale. The experience is like lying on our backs and looking at the stars: almost overwhelming.

So there is a kind of relief in turning to the remaining parts of the exhibition. Here too some elements are fixed: the Magna Carta material, which is very properly displayed, with the help of interactive gadgets and gizmos, to remind us all of our rights and obligations as citizens. The majority, however, are on a leisurely rotation which allows the library to demonstrate the depth of its holdings. When I last visited, in the early summer of 2010, the range of the literary material was as impressive as the depth. Among the earliest texts on view is a *Beowulf* manuscript – alongside some drafts of the great recent translation by Seamus Heaney, in which we can see him making shrewd adjustments to his own voice, in order to catch the voice of the poem. (In the opening line, "So the Spear Danes held sway once", that "once" becomes "in days gone by" – apparently more archaic, but crucially more definite too, and so in keeping with the clashing actualities of the poem.)

A sequence of marvels follows: a manuscript of poems by Sir Philip Sidney; John Milton's commonplace book; Jane Austen's little portable writing desk, given to her by her father in 1794; and the first draft of Thomas Hardy's *Tess of the d'Urbervilles* (1888), with its original chapter titles neatly crossed out, so you can see how posterity was denied the very suggestive "Her Education. The Maiden".

These lead into the modern age, where we find an engrossing gathering of material by Isaac Rosenberg, one of the most heart-wringing of the war poets, and swiftly on to our own time: a manuscript by Ted Hughes of a poem that eventually made its way into *Birthday Letters* (then entitled "The Sorrows of the Deer"), a wonderfully complicated page of the novelist Angela Carter, and a sample from the Ballard archive: the opening page of *Crash*.

Listed end to end like this, things can lose their sense of uniqueness. But one of the great pleasures of the Ritblat Gallery lies in discovering how individual character asserts itself in order to achieve its ambitions. Rosenberg's poem "Break of Day in the Trenches", in which the remarkable phrase "a queer sardonic rat" replaces "a queer uncanny rat", is a little masterpiece of visual arrangement: the distinctly sculptural handwriting seems to hew the poem out of the air. Hughes's poem is written in a script that looks like the prints of birds' feet in wet concrete. And Ballard's text, in which handwritten amendments swarm across the original typescript, is so piled up and crossed through, it becomes a kind of crash itself – from which flows prose of exceptional lucidity and directness.

"Infinite riches in a little room": the Renaissance description of a sonnet could equally well apply to the Ritblat. It is a place where the traditional expectations of libraries are matched by those we associate with galleries – visual elements form a link with meaningful ones, to create an overall effect that is bigger than both. So the place creates in us a strange mixture of inwardness and outwardness – a self-scrutiny, whether we are writers or not, as well as a curiosity about others.

This in turn leads to a further paradox. We leave the collection thinking that we have made contact across the centuries with people whose work in one way or another has been vital to us, because they form a part of our religious faith, or they have brightened our imaginative lives, or we have been mesmerised by their authors. This breeds a sense of intimacy, consolidated by the sense that as we look at the literary documents (less so the religious texts) we are looking over the author's shoulder. And yet at the same time the documents retain a bewitching otherness. They celebrate the difference of other minds, as well as their familiarity – and they raise questions. How do we make our mark by making marks? What is created by genius, and what derives from work? What is the relationship between the two? And what is the relationship between the sublime and the everyday? The questions hang in the air long after we have returned to plain daylight.

The Sir John Ritblat Treasures Gallery
The British Library, 96 Euston Road, London NW1 2DB, UK
www.bl.uk

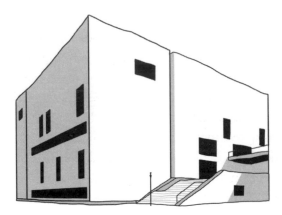

A Debt to Rudolf Leopold

LEOPOLD MUSEUM, VIENNA

William Boyd

Forty years ago, I was sitting my art A-level and dreaming of becoming a painter. My constant book of reference was *A Dictionary of Modern Painting*, published by Methuen: 400 pages of eclectic scholarship, from Apollinaire to Zandomeneghi, with contributions from 30 eminent art historians. I still have the book in its 1964 edition, and there is no entry for Egon Schiele. He doesn't even appear in the entry on the Viennese Secession or the one on Oskar Kokoschka, his exact contemporary. His solitary mention occurs in the piece on Gustav Klimt, where it is noted, in passing, that "Klimt was much admired by E. Schiele".

I cite all this both to illustrate the vagaries of art history and to show the comparatively recent nature of Schiele's now vast reputation. His work is reproduced everywhere and known to a huge public, and his critical standing now overshadows both Klimt's and Kokoschka's. This is due to the efforts of one man, the art historian and collector Rudolf Leopold.

Born in 1925, Leopold began buying the work of Schiele (and some of the other artists of the Viennese Secession school) in the 1950s – an astute move of unrivalled prescience – steadily building up the largest collection of Schiele's paintings and drawings in the world. Leopold was then a young ophthalmologist of modest means – no art-loving plutocrat – and his passionate collecting was a straightforward labour of love. His publication of

Schiele's catalogue raisonné in 1972 probably marks the beginning of Schiele's rapid ascent to artistic prominence.

This must have been the time when I first became aware of Schiele – I remember buying postcards and a small monograph of reproductions while I was at university. I became utterly compelled by the Schiele style, with its jagged, graphic elongations, its mannered distortions, and for a couple of years I tried to draw like Schiele – and failed, of course (dreams of being an artist not entirely moribund). However, he has remained for me one of the permanent artists in my personal pantheon.

This largely explains why the Leopold Museum in Vienna is my favourite art gallery: not only does it house the world's outstanding collection of Schiele's work – with many masterworks on its walls – but it is also, haphazardly and wholly inadvertently, a storehouse of my own youthful ambitions to live the life of an artist. Seeing Schiele's work acts as a kind of infallible Proustian trigger for me, providing a fast rewind to my teenage years and their fervid dreams. Whenever I'm in Vienna I visit it, even for ten minutes or so, and it never fails to entrance and to delight, and, because the hang of Rudolf Leopold's collection is forever changing in subtle ways, there is always some new revelation.

For example, when I went back to Vienna and the Leopold Museum for this article there was a room full of Schiele's landscapes, many of which I had not seen before, and landscape is not a form of painting one immediately associates with him. That March day in Vienna was cool and sunny and the gallery itself – a great square creamy-stone art bunker, set in its corner of the Museumsquartier's huge courtyard – was looking massive and secure, as if it had always been there. I always try to imagine what it must be like for Rudolf Leopold to have his "own" museum, to see his name carved on its limestone façade. It was

opened in 2001, funded by the Austrian state and designed by
the architects Laurids and Manfred Ortner. It stands as the most
extraordinary vindication of one man's personal taste and dedi-
cation and it is an extra frisson to think that Rudolf Leopold
has an office in the building and is still actively involved in its
exhibitions, acquisitions and administration. And one can't
help fantasising further, wondering – if shades existed – what
the shade of Egon Schiele would be feeling if he could see his
immortality thus enshrined …

Schiele's short, tormented life has its own bitter and dark
romance. This amazingly gifted young artist, born in 1890, was
nurtured in the spirit of Austria's Secession movement – a rejec-
tion of the Beaux-Arts classic style and the stuffy mediocrity
of the salons. He was inspired by Klimt's decorative eroticism
and, in the first decade of the 20th century, turned it into a form
of daring, expressionistic figuration – supercharging it in the
process. The work Schiele produced in the last ten years of his
life was as powerful and individual as late Van Gogh: it was as if
Arthur Rimbaud had turned painter.

The outrage and bourgeois horror provoked by the overt
carnality of his skinny, distorted male and female nudes was
predictable; prosecution for perversion of minors less so. In 1912
Schiele, then living in a small provincial town, made the mistake
of inviting pubescent girls to his studio and using them as his
nude models. He was eventually acquitted of child abuse but
found guilty of having erotic images around children and imprisoned for 24 days. The experience had a profound and disturbing
effect on him.

Despite this scandal, by the end of the first world war his reputation was growing and he was just beginning to be spoken of
as the natural heir to Gustav Klimt when the 1918 flu pandemic

claimed in October, first, the life of his heavily pregnant wife, Edith, and then, three days later, the artist's own. Egon Schiele was dead and forgotten at 28, but with an astonishing body of work behind him, waiting for Rudolf Leopold to discover it and present it to the world.

The Leopold Museum itself is purpose-built and something of an illusion. From the outside it appears impregnable, almost fortress-like with its high stone façade pierced with the occasional asymmetrical windows. However, inside there is a wide, tall, glass-roofed atrium, with the galleries set out on all four sides around it. On the upper floors huge plate-glass windows look out over the roofscapes of old Vienna and you can see the towers of the Rathaus and the domes of the Hofburg. The atrium is a beautiful, empty space. On the day I was there the sunlight shone through the glass roof creating lucent abstract patterns on the sheer limestone interior walls. In fact you could go as far as saying that the atrium interior of the Leopold Museum, in certain lights, is something of a work of art itself, a luminescent installation, the stone walls containing a refulgent volume of air.

But it's what is hanging in the galleries that lures you away. Reproductions are wonderful – and all very well – but there is nothing like seeing famous works of art up close, in the real. Schiele's famous *Seated Male Nude* of 1910 is a case in point. The first thing that startles is its scale – just bigger than life-size. As with many of Schiele's paintings, a form of thought experiment is required to try and imagine the effect of seeing them when they were first displayed. This gaunt full-frontal nude self-portrait, its skin hued in bilious tones of green and yellow, stylised and footless, with its orange-red nipples and one red eye, must have seemed like some kind of terrifying apparition. Indeed, the same shock effect is true of all of Schiele's portraits: skin is rendered with shades of blue or scumbled rose, the eyes start, wide and exophthalmic, staring out at the viewer. They are as starkly powerful as anything by Francis Bacon or Lucian Freud – and they were painted about half a century earlier.

Two small self-portraits sit adjacently in the right angle of a wall of one gallery, almost facing each other, inadvertently depicting the Jekyll and Hyde character of Schiele and his art. One – constantly reproduced – is the serenely knowing *Self-Portrait with Winter Cherry* (1912). The other is *Self-Portrait with Head Inclined* (1912). This second one is masterfully rendered: the painting of the face and the hand is thin, oil paint made semi-transparent with turpentine, contrasted with the thick impasto white of the shirt and background.

Most unusually, Schiele has a moustache in this portrait – the only image of him moustachioed that I can recall. Luckily for posterity, Schiele was fond of being photographed and in all the many photographs we have of him he appears cleanshaven. I don't mean to be facetious, but Austro-Hungarian Vienna was, among everything else, the city of facial hair. Was it a mark of rebellion not to grow a beard or a moustache in those days and thus distinguish yourself from the hirsute complacent burghers and whiskered bemedalled soldiers? I think of another of Schiele's Vienna contemporaries, another harbinger of the modern 20th century and a ground-breaker in his field, the philosopher Ludwig Wittgenstein – lean, ascetic and permanently clean-shaven, like Schiele. Does the demonic stare in this portrait, the added black stripe of the moustache, gesture towards the schizophrenic nature of Viennese society in those days before the Great War? This may be the wisdom of hindsight but another contemporary of Schiele (and of Wittgenstein and Freud) in pre-war Vienna was Adolf Hitler, then an embittered and near-destitute down-and-out, roaming the streets, living in squalid hostels, nurturing his paranoid fantasies. Twenty years later he would be chancellor of Germany.

If Schiele's Mr Hyde persona can be found in his near-pornographic nudes and contorted, emaciated figures with their skull-heads, then his gentler Dr Jekyll self can be seen in his landscapes and townscapes and his still-lifes – particularly in his drawings. Schiele was a marvellously gifted draughtsman and the confidence of his graphic line is remarkable. It's interesting to contrast Schiele's drawings with Klimt's, also on display in the Leopold Museum. Set Schiele's dark, assured, emphatic pencil sketches beside Klimt's fine, tentative, wispy, evanescent drawings and you see the two distinct artistic personalities rendered immediately visible.

The Leopold is a sizeable museum – it has rooms devoted to furniture and design as well as its collection of Schiele, Klimt and other Austrian artists of that generation – but one of its attractions is its scale. It does not daunt or induce art-fatigue; its delights can be savoured in a morning or an afternoon. To this degree it reminds me of another favourite museum of mine – the Whitney on Madison Avenue in New York – again solidly modern and streamlined in design but accessible and containable. The Whitney was named after Gertrude Vanderbilt Whitney, but what it doesn't possess is the presiding presence of its founder and its founder's collection that the Leopold so effectively and entrancingly displays.

And of course you step out of the modern Whitney into the brash modernity of Manhattan. The Leopold's huge and unspoken asset is its context in the ancient city of Vienna, that astonishingly beautiful and well-preserved haven of centuries of culture. Vienna has sometimes been dubbed "Gesamtkunstwerk

Wien". The Leopold Museum deserves that title also – a total work of art.

Leopold Museum
Museumsplatz 1, A 1070 Vienna, Austria
www.leopoldmuseum.org

Thank You for the Music

ABBA: THE MUSEUM, STOCKHOLM

Matthew Sweet

A basement in Stockholm. A tomato-red plastic telephone mounted on a pedestal. Behind it, a wall-size photograph depicting two women and two men. Young, cheerful, pristine – and known throughout the world as the blonde one, the brunette, the one with the beard and the one without the beard. Bolted above this, an official-looking sign with a message in urgent upper-case italics, hinting that in the advent of some distinctly Scandinavian catastrophe – the coming of Ragnarök, the fall of the great tree of Yggdrasil – help would be at hand. "Om telefonen ringer, svara, de at abba som ringer!"

I know what you're thinking. Where are the faience ushabti? The fragile Venetian tapestries? The photographs of a Booker winner in a reverie before a vitrine of Meissen ware? And hang on – isn't that the helicopter from the cover of *Arrival*? Surely this writer has misunderstood the brief. What next for these pages? Madame Tussaud's? Planet Hollywood? Peppa Pig World?

On Djurgården, the greenest of Stockholm's 14 islands, you can gaze upon the carcass of the Vasa, the 17th-century warship that cruised straight into the realm of the symbolic by sinking 1,300 metres into its maiden voyage. Or you can wander through the zoological gardens and open-air architectural archive of Skansen, where the wooden spire of an 18th-century church soars skywards and wolves howl at the milky dusk. Or you can turn your back on these phenomena, and examine what lies beneath a squat yellow building beside the ferry terminal.

ABBA: The Museum opened in May 2013 as a monument to the lives and work of Sweden's four most successful pop stars – Agnetha Fältskog, Björn Ulvaeus, Benny Andersson and Anni-Frid Lyngstad. Quite a mouthful, which is why their manager, Stig Anderson, condensed it to an acronym – after first checking that Sweden's biggest herring-pickling company didn't mind sharing the name.

Some of the space is occupied by larky hands-on exhibits. A bank of faders allows you to reconstruct the mix of "Fernando". A row of recording booths is busy with headphone-wearing visitors belting "The Winner Takes It All" into unwired mikes. And a curtained anteroom contains the museum's equivalent of the Chamber of Horrors – a device that scans your face and appends it to the bodies of a computer-generated Abba line-up.

As well as a playground, however, this is also a reliquary. Behind the glass panels lie Benny's silver platform shoes, the Telex machine that spewed out some of Abba's most lucrative contracts, a tea-chest bass twanged by Björn in his skiffle period, a Star Trek expanse of mixing desk extracted from the Polar recording studios, those sateen blouses worn by Agnetha and Anni-Frid when they sang "Waterloo" back to back at the Brighton Dome, and won the 1974 Eurovision song contest. (Come close, and you can see that they are studded with little enamel badges bearing the faces of Stan Laurel and his 1920s rival Harry Langdon.)

The sceptical eye might dismiss it as the unlovely detritus of Europop – a subterranean fire-trap of hen-night kitsch. But this would be to underestimate the semiotic thickness of Abba's art – and trust me, you really wouldn't want to do that. The artefacts on display evoke, sometimes painfully, the band's personal and artistic trajectory: the vanishing grins, the collapsing marriages, the tour-bus melancholia, their progress towards that bleak and clear-eyed final album, *The Visitors* – their *Winterreise*. It's true that Abba lyrics sometimes exhibit errors familiar to EFL teachers around the world ("since many years I haven't seen a rifle in your hand," says the narrator of "Fernando"), but who else could have produced a song like their last recorded work, "The Day Before You Came" – an account of joy measured in the minutiae of depression, and possibly the only pop song ever written in the past-modal perfect tense? ("I'm sure I had my dinner watching something on TV," reflects Agnetha. "There's not, I think, a single episode of *Dallas* that I didn't see.")

This is not the special pleading of an obsessive. I know what it is to be a fan. Ladies and gentlemen of the jury, I possess three pairs of Dalek socks, and when my children were asked to draw a phrenological diagram of my head, both reserved a fist-sized hunk for matters pertaining to *Doctor Who*. No Abba zone was demarcated – as far as they're concerned, Abba are YouTube stars who belong to them, not me. Until the *Abba Gold* compilation appeared in 1992, I'd never owned one of their albums. The nearest I'd come was in 1980, the year I played for the worst lacrosse team in the north-west of England, when I bought, on my way to a 16–0 defeat in Blackpool, a disc-shaped bubblegum slipped inside a perfect miniature replica of the sleeve of "Super Trouper". After our customary humiliation, the coach drove us home in silence. Abba's latest hit came on the radio. We were, I recall, sick and tired of everything.

In those days, though, no purchase was necessary. Abba's songs and their attendant sensibility were part of the warp and weft of the culture. My first clear memory of hearing them dates from October 1976, when the wave-crash of notes that begins

"Dancing Queen" blasted from the speakers at Hull Fair and provided the soundtrack to a painful incident of childhood loss – my letting go of what is probably best described as a racist helium balloon, and watching its surprised expression recede to a black dot high above Humberside. Fifteen years later, when I bailed out of university for a year in order to avoid a former girlfriend, I found myself selling ice-cream in front of *Chess*, Benny's and Björn's cold-war musical – whose company manager seemed to regard the recent fall of the Berlin Wall as a calculated assault on the box office. In the last lecture I had attended before making my retreat, I'd listened to Terry Eagleton poke fun at fellow Marxists who had "woken up one morning and found they had been hermeneutic materialists all along". No such strategy was available to the characters of *Chess*. How lost they seemed, personally, in their unhappy love affairs, and politically, in an ideological world that, on the other side of the proscenium, had dismantled itself shortly before the opening night.

Which brings me to another claim. My first visit to the Abba museum was made in close proximity to a trip to Washington, DC, where, at the Smithsonian Museum of American History, I'd peered at the rifles discharged during the Kent State massacre and the wreck of a filing cabinet crowbarred by the White House Plumbers. And it seemed to me that Abba's effects were artefacts of a comparable order.

Abba didn't ask to take part in the culture wars, but the barrage happened just the same. On the night they won the Eurovision Song Contest, the audience in the Brighton Dome came roaring to their feet, but the Swedes were less impressed. After walking from the venue in a daze of pleasure, Stig Anderson found himself on camera with Ulf Gudmundson, a Swedish television reporter garlanded for documentaries such as "Northern

Ireland – from the Crusades to the Class Struggle". Instead of offering his congratulations, Gudmundson asked Stig to justify writing an up-tempo, glam-rock love song about a battle in which 40,000 troops were slaughtered. Anderson's reply? "Go to hell before an accident happens."

In the 1960s and 1970s, Sweden was another word for utopia – particularly in countries afflicted by industrial decline and rising unemployment. The Swedish Model, as it was called without a hint of double entendre, seemed to have delivered the Swedes from anxiety. They had the highest living standards in Europe. They had big cars and modernist furniture. Their welfare state seemed a miracle of generosity – this was a country without visible deprivation. Their political neutrality gave them moral independence, too. How many other states would have invited Bertrand Russell and Jean Paul Sartre to convene a war crimes tribunal that judged America guilty of genocide in Vietnam? "When a napalm bomb explodes among innocent civilians," Olof Palme, the prime minister, told the Swedish parliament, "it is a defeat for the idea of democracy." (When Washington heard that, it brought home its ambassador.)

With this came a measure of cultural puritanism. One of its strongest embodiments was a musical movement called progg – which, unlike its Anglophone namesake, was not interested in the production of four-hour symphonic concept albums about Orcs, but busied itself making coarse, punky, socialist folk music. Progg and its fans hated Abba, and hated its manager even more. "He is dangerous," said Lars Forsell, one of Sweden's leading poets, "and what he writes is shit." The media agreed. Its response to Abba's success was, briefly, to abolish the pop charts and cancel the Stockholm equivalent of *Top of the Pops*. Swedish television couldn't wriggle out of its duty to stage the 1975 Eurovision Song

Contest, but made its feelings known by giving more attention to a musical counter-demonstration than the official event. "For leftists in Sweden in the Seventies," reflected Björn, "we became the Antichrist." And the personal, Abba discovered, was the political. When they invited the Sierra Leonean drummer Ahmadu Jarr to play with them, he declined, explaining that his wife would leave him if he accepted the gig.

Today, Sweden's ideological landscape looks very different. Progg is the preserve of nostalgic connoisseurs. The social model constructed in the days of Olof Palme has gone, though not so suddenly and inexplicably as Palme himself. (His assassination, 20 years ago, remains an unsolved case.) Swedish asylum policy is among the most liberal in Europe – but the far right, in the form of Jimmie Åkesson's Sweden Democrats, is now the third-biggest party in the Riksdag.

Abba's position has also changed. In the 1970s, the New Left held them in contempt. Today, the band's male alumni are engaged in a quiet campaign against the Nordic New Right. When the youth wing of the anti-immigration Danish People's Party turned Abba's 1975 hit "Mamma Mia" into a hymn to its leader, Pia Kjaersgaard, Benny and Björn called in the lawyers. When Gudrun Schyman, a former leader of one of Sweden's communist groups, co-founded the women's party Feminist Initiative, Benny became one of its biggest donors. During the 2014 election campaign I went down to the square in central Stockholm where every party maintains a little wooden hut in which voters can meet the candidates and read their literature. Most of the activity here seemed dour and dutiful – but in the glossy pink FI hut, they were having the time of their lives. Their enthusiasm, unfortunately, did not translate into parliamentary seats.

You couldn't construct a coherent philosophical universe

from the work of Abba. Not quite. But the world observed through the lens of their songs often seems a coldly deterministic place – one where human agency is frail and inadequate. "The Winner Takes It All" posits a cosmos in which we are subject to the whims of dice-playing gods – Scandi cousins, surely, of the beings mentioned in *King Lear* and *Tess of the d'Urbervilles*. That history book on the shelf, insists "Waterloo", is always repeating itself.

In the Abba museum, there's a little area that represents "Knowing Me, Knowing You" – the first of the band's songs about divorce, written by Björn when his marriage to Agnetha was entering its terminal phase. It's a 1970s kitchen, somewhere in Swedish suburbia. On the table, there's a half-eaten bowl of muesli. A child has just left for school. A wintry view is visible through the pine framed window. There is, says the lyric, nothing we can do.

"If the telephone rings", reads the sign above the tomato-red telephone, "pick it up, it's Abba calling." And it ain't no lie. The only people who have the number are Agnetha Fältskog, Björn Ulvaeus, Benny Andersson and Anni-Frid Lyngstad. But if it did ring, what could they say? It's all in their songs, in the harmonies of their voices, in the image of a landscape in winter.

ABBA: The Museum
Djurgårdsvägen 68, Stockholm, Sweden
www.abbathemuseum.com

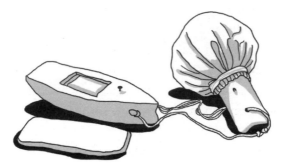

Glasgow's Palace of Dreams

KELVINGROVE, GLASGOW

Andrew O'Hagan

The Scottish novelist and artist Alasdair Gray once remarked that if the place you live in isn't painted, if your voices aren't heard on the radio and your people never appear in novels, then you may live there in real time but you don't live there imaginatively. I grew up outside Glasgow in a Catholic household full of voices, stories and strong beliefs, but my parents didn't have books. If you grow up in a house like that, where classical music is never heard and painting is for ever a matter of Dulux, you may come to adulthood wondering whether high culture isn't something that can only describe the lives of others.

One morning in May 1981, when I was 13, I went into the city and found my way to Kelvingrove. It had beautiful red sandstone, and daylight glinted off the arched windows. I was nervous going in: I wasn't sure if you had to pay, or whether you had to know something already. But when I climbed the stairs and looked over the balcony, I had what I can only describe as my first teenage epiphany: this was ours, all ours, the paintings, the light, the stonework. It belonged to the people of Glasgow, and to me.

I made my way to the end of a corridor, where Salvador Dalí's *Christ of St John of the Cross* hung in theatrical gloom. I was used to crucifixion scenes. (My grandmother, who ran a fish shop, once pointed to a poster of Jesus in his crown of thorns, pinned on the shop wall. "Mind yourself," she said. "That's what happened to him for being good!") Only when I saw the Dalí did I rethink my sacramental hours as problems of light and form, seeing the question of devotion as a creative issue. I was familiar with the pallid image of Christ as a dying everyman, a bearded, etiolated figure, eyes rolling heavenward in his Passion. But Dalí doesn't show the face. We see a healthy man in his prime hanging crucified in cinematic light, hovering mysteriously over Galilee as if remembering earthly goodness. I sat opposite the picture for a long time, and when I stood up, I wasn't the same.

Kelvingrove opened in 1902. The Lord Provost described it then as "a palace of dreams", and that's what it has always been, a building filled with the ghosts of artistic possibility. Bequests to the museum have long been a matter of honour in Glasgow. Archibald McLellan gave a Titian, *The Adulteress Brought before Christ*, a Botticelli and more, and many have followed him. On subsequent visits, I got to know the taste of a certain Glasgow collector, William McInnes, who, in 1944, gave a Van Gogh, a Picasso, a stunning Monet and a work by Henri Matisse that may be imprinted on my dreams long after death. *The Pink Tablecloth* is a work of such sublime decorative harmony that it seems to set the tone for the whole museum. It does this in more ways than one, for the best of the Scottish paintings at Kelvingrove take their cue from works like these by Matisse. Above all, for a boy searching for local miracles, it was the Scottish Colourists that fixed the museum in my mind. It was marvellous, of course, to see a Titian, but the brazen works of these Edwardian stylists – Cadell, Fergusson, Peploe, Hunter – cemented in my mind the idea that a great museum is not just a repository of treasures but an instigator of vision.

At the close of *Our Fathers*, my first novel, the narrator, Jamie, is sitting on the bed with his grandmother, Margaret, looking at some prints. One of them is Cadell's *The Red Chair*. "Jesus, Mary and Joseph," says Margaret, who grew up in the Highlands. "These are the very best pictures I ever saw. You can't get over them. Look, Jamie. These are the pictures that brought me south." When I wrote those lines, I was thinking of my own journey towards Cadell and the rest of the paintings in the museum at Kelvingrove. To me, those works seemed to possess magical modern properties: it was as if, viewed on days when I bunked off school, they held the secret of our potential to grow up and see the world fresh.

When I travelled back to Kelvingrove recently – not, like Margaret, travelling south, but north from London – I tried to work out what it was about the Colourists that had so captured my belief. The pictures are often of quite anodyne things – ladies in wide hats, scenes of the Hebrides in sun and rain. Easy subjects, in a way. But it was the style that got me. These were men who'd grown up with their fair share of the grey and mundane, but they went to France and came back iridescent. I loved the notion that a human imagination is not a static thing; that a zone of excellence such as impressionist France is not a stymied local repast but a movable feast. You go away to come home.

Returns to museums can then be like the fulfilment of a Proustian contract. The objects themselves have travelled with you but the smell of the floors, the feel of the marble, this is the stuff of old acquaintance. And then before me was Francis Cadell's large *Interior – The Orange Blind*. There she is, the woman sitting on the green chaise, her white face eternally mysterious. A man plays a piano in the shadows behind her, the side of the piano looking warm from the light filtered through the orange blind. And in front of the lady are the teapot and the cups, all of it redolent of an elegant moment that only exists in paint.

I saw the Dalí again and wondered if it hadn't grown in

spiritual majesty as my own faith declined. I learned something I hadn't known: the painting was damaged one day by a man with mental-health issues who threw a stone at it and ripped the canvas, saying such a painting had no business being in the collection at Kelvingrove. I paused over that. Maybe that's what a great museum does to us: makes us possessive, makes us think we know it too well. I don't mind rooms set out by period, but I always want to run away when I see themed rooms in a museum. Kelvingrove hasn't escaped all that: "Creatures of the Past" is a little touchy-feely; "Conflict and Consequence" shows a little dab of post-colonial thinking.

But it's still a palace of dreams. I wonder what children in the age of the internet make of St Kilda mailboats, these small wooden vessels that were crafted by the people of St Kilda to carry letters (and money for postage) to the mainland in the hope that they might make it to the addressee. Before a steamboat service came in 1877, St Kildans had no way of communicating with the world, and so they set these tiny wooden boats afloat across the sea with messages folded inside. They sent them off as we would ping an e-mail, minus the certainty, the thoughtlessness or the speed. The St Kilda mailboats tell a story of how we have moved beyond the world's power to delay us.

Kelvingrove was always about progress. The idea of opening it came to fruition during the huge International Exhibition in Kelvingrove Park in 1888. (That was a big year for pride and self-consciousness in Glasgow: Celtic Football Club was founded and work began on Templeton's carpet factory, both still standing.) And as I walked through the museum I felt I wasn't just visiting objects and paintings I loved, but walking through an idea of civic awakening.

In Glasgow the civic always feels personal. Kelvingrove may

have been built to resemble the great church of Santiago de Compostela. It may have works by Turner and Van Gogh. But it will always be the creak of the vernacular that sounds as you walk over its several floors. My mind was still ablaze with the Scottish Colourists when I returned to the ground floor and saw the painting of Anna Pavlova by Sir John Lavery that stands just under two metres high. Orange scarf thrown above her head, weight tilted back, Pavlova is the very image of vigour across the distance of a century or so. And yet, this being Glasgow, my eye kept returning to the painter's surname. My grandmother, the one with the fish shop, was called Molly Lavery. Her father played football for Clyde; her uncle Robert died on the Somme. They had no books or pictures in the house either, but they liked to think that their kinsman John Lavery was out capturing the world for Glasgow, and occasionally capturing Glasgow for the world.

Kelvingrove
Argyle Street, Glasgow G3 8AG, UK
www.glasgowlife.org.uk/museums/kelvingrove

About the authors

Julian Barnes is the author of twelve novels, including *The Sense of an Ending*, which won the 2011 Man Booker Prize for Fiction, and the *Sunday Times* number-one bestseller *The Noise of Time*. He has also written three books of short stories, *Cross Channel*, *The Lemon Table* and *Pulse*; four collections of essays; and two books of non-fiction, *Nothing To Be Frightened Of* and *Levels of Life*. His work has been translated into 47 languages.

William Boyd is a novelist and screenwriter. He has published fourteen novels, the latest being *Sweet Caress* (Bloomsbury). He has written widely on art and artists over the years, most notably in his short "biography", *Nat Tate: an American Artist 1928–1960*.

John Burnside is a novelist, short story writer and poet. His poetry collection *Black Cat Bone* won both the Forward Prize and the T. S. Eliot Prize in 2011. His memoir *A Lie About My Father* won the Saltire Society Scottish Book of the Year Award and Scottish Arts Council Non-Fiction Book of the Year; his story collection *Something Like Happy* received the 2014 Edge Hill Prize. He writes a monthly nature column for *New Statesman* and is a regular contributor to *London Review of Books*. His book on 20th-century poetry, *The Music of Time*, will be published by Profile Books in 2018.

Frank Cottrell-Boyce is a children's novelist and screenwriter. His first book, *Millions*, won the Carnegie Medal and was made into a film by Danny Boyle, with whom Frank also collaborated on the opening ceremony of the 2012 Olympic Games. His latest book is *Sputnik's Guide to Life*. He is Professor of Reading at Liverpool Hope University.

Roddy Doyle is the author of ten novels, two collections of stories, two books of dialogues and *Rory & Ita*, a memoir of his parents. He co-wrote *The Second Half* with Roy Keane. He has written eight books for children. He won the Booker Prize in 1993 for *Paddy Clarke Ha Ha Ha*. He has also written for stage and screen. His translation of Mozart's *Don Giovanni* premiered in Dublin in September 2016.

Margaret Drabble, DBE, novelist and critic, was born in Sheffield and educated at the Mount School, York and Newnham College, Cambridge. Her first novel, *A Summer Bird-Cage* (1963), was followed by eighteen others, most recently *The Dark Flood Rises* (2016). A volume of short stories, *A Day in the Life of a Smiling Woman*, was published in 2011. She edited two editions of the *Oxford Companion to English Literature* (1985 and 2000) and has written biographies of Arnold Bennett (1974) and Angus Wilson (1995). She is married to the biographer Michael Holroyd.

Aminatta Forna is a fiction writer and essayist and the award-winning author of the three novels *The Hired Man*, *The Memory of Love* and *Ancestor Stones*, and the memoir *The Devil that Danced on the Water*. She is winner of a Windham Campbell Prize and the Commonwealth Writers Best Book Prize, among others, and a finalist for the Orange Prize, IMPAC, Samuel Johnson, BBC Short Story Prize and Neustadt prizes. She is currently a Lannan Visiting Chair of Poetics at Georgetown University in Washington, DC.

Alan Hollinghurst is the author of five novels: *The Swimming-Pool Library*, *The Folding Star*, *The Spell*, *The Line of Beauty* and *The Stranger's Child*. He has received the Somerset Maugham Award, the James Tait Black Memorial Prize for Fiction and the 2004 Man Booker Prize. He lives in London.

John Lanchester is a journalist and novelist. His journalism has appeared in *Granta*, the *New York Review of Books*, the *Guardian* and the *New Yorker*, among other publications. His first novel, *The Debt to Pleasure*, won the 1996 Whitbread Book Award in the First Novel category. His memoir *Family Romance* (2006) recounts the story of his mother, an ex-nun who concealed her real name, age and life story from her husband and son. On the publication of *How to Speak Money* (2014), Michael Lewis described Lanchester as 'one of the great explainers of the financial crash and its aftermath'.

Claire Messud is the author of four novels and a book of novellas. *The Emperor's Children*, translated into over twenty languages, was named one of the *New York Times*'s Ten Best Books in 2006. Her most recent novel is *The Woman Upstairs* (2013). A regular contributor to the *New York Review of Books*, the *New York Times Book Review* and the *Financial Times*, among other publications, Messud teaches at Harvard University and lives with her family in Cambridge, MA.

A. D. Miller's first novel, *Snowdrops*, was shortlisted for the Man Booker prize and numerous other awards. His other books are *The Faithful Couple* and *The Earl of Petticoat Lane*, a memoir of immigration, the Blitz and the underwear industry. He has written introductions to novellas by Tolstoy and Dostoyevsky for Hesperus Classics. As Moscow correspondent of *The Economist*, he travelled widely across the former Soviet Union; he is currently the magazine's Southern correspondent, based in Atlanta, Georgia.

Michael Morpurgo began writing stories in the early 1970s and was appointed Children's Laureate in 2003. He has written over 130 books, including *The Butterfly Lion, Kensuke's Kingdom, Why the Whales Came, The Mozart Question, Shadow* and *War Horse,* which was adapted for a hugely successful stage production by the National Theatre in London and then, in 2011, for a film directed by Steven Spielberg. His book *Private Peaceful* has been adapted for the stage by Simon Reade and has now been made into a film, directed by Pat O'Connor. Michael was awarded the OBE for his writing in 2006.

Andrew Motion was the UK Poet Laureate from 1999 to 2009. He is now Homewood Professor in the Arts at Johns Hopkins University and lives in Baltimore.

Andrew O'Hagan is one of his generation's most exciting and most serious chroniclers of contemporary Britain. He has been nominated three times for the Man Booker Prize. He was voted one of *Granta*'s Best of Young British Novelists in 2003. He has won the *Los Angeles Times* Book Award and the E. M. Forster Award from the American Academy of Arts & Letters. He lives in London.

Alice Oswald studied Classics at Oxford and then trained as a gardener. In 1996 she published her first book of poems, *The Thing in the Gap-Stone Stile*. She was writer in residence at Dartington Hall from 1996 to 1998 and there wrote her long poem *Dart*, which won the T. S. Eliot Prize in 2002. Other collections have won the inaugural Ted Hughes Award, the Hawthornden Prize and the Warwick Prize. In 2009 she won a Cholmondeley award for her contribution to poetry. She is married with three children and lives in Devon.

Ann Patchett is the author of three works of non-fiction and seven novels, most recently *Commonwealth*. She is the winner of the Orange Prize in the UK and the PEN/Faulkner Award in the US. Her novel *Bel Canto* has been translated into more than thirty languages and was recently staged at the Lyric Opera of Chicago. She lives in Nashville, Tennessee, where she is the co-owner of Parnassus Books.

Don Paterson is a Scottish poet, writer and musician. His first collection of poetry, *Nil Nil* (1993), won the Forward Prize for Best First Collection. *God's Gift to Women* (1997) won the T. S. Eliot Prize and the Geoffrey Faber Memorial Prize. *Landing Light* (2003) won the T. S. Eliot Prize and the Whitbread Poetry Award. He was appointed OBE in 2008, and was awarded the Queen's Gold Medal for Poetry in 2010.

Allison Pearson is a novelist and journalist. Her bestselling novel *I Don't Know How She Does It* (2002) was made into a movie of the same name starring Sarah Jessica Parker. *I Think I Love You*, her second novel, was published in 2010. She has written for the *Daily Mail*, the *Evening Standard* and the *Independent*, and is a columnist at the *Daily Telegraph*.

Ali Smith was born in Inverness in 1962 and lives in Cambridge. She is a writer of novels, short stories, plays and criticism. Her latest novel, *How to Be Both*, was shortlisted for the 2014 Man

Booker Prize and won the Bailey's Women's Prize for Fiction, the Goldsmiths Prize, the Costa Novel Award and the Saltire Society's Literary Book of the Year Award. Her story collection, *Public Library and Other Stories*, was published in November 2015, and her novel *Autumn* was published by Penguin Hamish Hamilton in 2016.

Rory Stewart was briefly a soldier, and then a diplomat. Between 2000 and 2002 he walked 6,000 miles across Asia. He then served as a coalition deputy-governor in the Marsh Arab regions of Iraq. In 2005 he moved to Afghanistan, where he established the Turquoise Mountain Foundation. At the end of 2008 he became a Professor at Harvard University's Kennedy School. At the time of writing, he was an MP and the Minister of the Environment in the UK government. His books are the *New York Times* bestseller *The Places in Between*, *The Prince of the Marshes* and *Can Intervention Work?* (with Gerald Knaus).

Matthew Sweet is author of *Inventing the Victorians* (2001), *Shepperton Babylon* (2005) and *The West End Front* (2011). A familiar voice in British broadcasting, he presents *Free Thinking* and *Sound of Cinema* on BBC Radio 3 and *The Philosopher's Arms* on BBC Radio 4. His journalism appears regularly in the *Guardian* and *Art Quarterly*. He has judged the Costa Book Award and edited *The Woman in White* for Penguin Classics, and is Series Consultant on the Showtime/Sky Atlantic series *Penny Dreadful*. In the BBC2 drama *An Adventure in Space and Time* he played a moth from the planet Vortis.

Jacqueline Wilson is one of Britain's bestselling authors, with more than 35 million books sold in the UK alone. She has been honoured with many prizes, including the Guardian Children's Fiction Award and the Children's Book of the Year. Jacqueline is a former Children's Laureate. She is Chancellor of the University of Roehampton, and in 2008 she was appointed DBE for services to children's literacy.

Tim Winton has published 26 books for adults and children, and his work has been translated into 28 languages. Since his first novel, *An Open Swimmer*, won the Australian Vogel Award in 1981, he has won the Miles Franklin Award four times (for *Shallows*, *Cloudstreet*, *Dirt Music* and *Breath*) and twice been shortlisted for the Booker Prize (for *The Riders* and *Dirt Music*). He lives in Western Australia.

Ann Wroe has been the Obituaries Editor of *The Economist* since 2003. After gaining a doctorate in medieval history, she worked at the BBC World Service, joining *The Economist* in 1976 to cover American politics. She has also written seven books. Her third book, *Pilate: The Biography of an Invented Man* (1999), was shortlisted for the Samuel Johnson Prize and the W. H. Smith Award; her sixth, *Orpheus: The Song of Life*, won the 2011 Criticos Prize. Her latest book is *Six Facets of Light*. She is a Fellow of the Royal Historical Society and of the Royal Society of Literature.

Illustrations

p. xvi – 'There's Life in These Walls' by Roddy Doyle (Lower East Side Tenement Museum, New York): exterior of the museum.

p. 10 – 'Rodin's Sonnets in Stone' by Allison Pearson (Musée Rodin, Paris): *The Kiss* by Auguste Rodin.

p. 18 – 'Cool Under Fire' by Rory Stewart (National Museum of Afghanistan, Kabul): Buddhist statue at Mes Aynak.

p. 26 – 'Cabinets of Wonder' by Frank Cottrell-Boyce (Pitt Rivers Museum, Oxford): toy made from an empty insecticide tin.

p. 32 – 'Painting in Stone' by Margaret Drabble (Museo dell'Opificio delle Pietre Dure, Florence): inlaid hard-stone table top.

p. 40 – 'Sanctum in the City' by Don Paterson (Frick Collection, New York): interior fountain court at the museum.

p. 50 – 'The Wings of Capri' by Ali Smith (Villa San Michele, Capri): statue of Mercury.

p. 60 – 'Spurned No Longer' by Tim Winton (National Gallery of Victoria, Melbourne): exterior of the museum (main entrance).

p. 70 – 'The Pity of War' by Michael Morpurgo (In Flanders Fields Museum, Ypres): first world war shell cases.

p. 80 – 'Love Bade Me Welcome' by Ann Patchett (Harvard Museum of Natural History, Cambridge, MA): glass flower by Leopold and/or Rudolf Blaschka.

p. 88 – 'A Plaster Cast in Copenhagen' by Alan Hollinghurst (Thorvaldsensmuseum, Copenhagen): exterior of the museum.

p. 98 – 'Palais of the Dolls' by Jacqueline Wilson (Musée de la Poupée, Paris): antique doll.

p. 108 – 'The Odessaphiles' by A. D. Miller (Odessa State Literary Museum, Odessa): interior of the museum (entrance hall and main staircase).

p. 118 – 'A Smiling Shrunken Goddess' by Alice Oswald (Corinium Museum, Cirencester): Roman bone figure of a water nymph.

p. 124 – 'Sons and Mothers' by John Burnside (Ensorhuis, Ostend): mask from the museum collection.

p. 134 – 'A Home from Home' by Claire Messud (Museum of Fine Arts, Boston): exterior of the museum.

p. 144 – 'Where Sibelius Fell Silent' by Julian Barnes (Ainola, Järvenpää): exterior of the museum.

p. 152 – 'Wordsworth's Continuous Force' by Ann Wroe (Dove Cottage, Grasmere): exterior of the museum.

p. 162 – 'Agony to Ecstasy' by John Lanchester (Prado, Madrid): *La Defensa de Zaragoza* by José Álvarez Cubero.

p. 170 – 'The Museum of Heartbreak' by Aminatta Forna (Museum of Broken Relationships, Zagreb): Ana's biker boots.

p. 179 – 'The Quiet Theatres' by Andrew Motion (Sir John Ritblat Treasures Gallery, London): illuminated English bible, 1537.

p. 188 – 'A Debt to Rudolf Leopold' by William Boyd (Leopold Museum, Vienna): exterior of the museum.

p. 196 – 'Thank You for the Music' by Matthew Sweet (ABBA: The Museum, Stockholm): the Abba hotline.

p. 204 – 'Glasgow's Palace of Dreams' by Andrew O'Hagan (Kelvingrove, Glasgow): nineteenth-century St Kilda mailboat.